What's Real About Race?

NORTON
SHORTS

What's Real About Race?

Untangling Science, Genetics, and Society

RINA BLISS

W. W. NORTON & COMPANY
Independent Publishers Since 1923

Manufacturing by Lakeside Book Company
Production manager: Delaney Adams

ISBN 978-1-324-02176-6

W. W. Norton & Company, Inc.
500 Fifth Avenue, New York, NY 10110
www.wwnorton.com

W. W. Norton & Company Ltd.
15 Carlisle Street, London W1D 3BS

10 9 8 7 6 5 4 3 2 1

For Luca, Mars, Rafa, and all the other
Alphas making us a better reality

CONTENTS

What's Real About Race?

INTRODUCTION

A S A CHILD, I WAS always confused by race. I was born and raised in Los Angeles, one of the most diverse places in the world. My mom immigrated there as a young woman from Jawa Timur, Indonesia. There she met my dad, who had come from New York to LA with his Ashkenazi Jewish family as a young boy. Inside our home, we enjoyed our unique tapestry of Bahasa Indonesia meets Yiddish language and culture, our batiks and Wayang puppets displayed proudly next to our Star of David. But outside our home, we were seen as a heterodox family marked by a fraught mixture of races. I lived in a city that increasingly celebrated being "browner" and more *mestizo* or "multiracial" than the rest of the United States, thanks to its rich Latin culture and civil rights history. Still, I somehow felt at the core of my being that our version of blending was utterly wrong.

My preschool friends, whose parents came from all reaches of the globe, made fun of my mom's culture and her accent. By four, I got used to my peers adoring those who spoke Spanish (or Spanglish), while ostracizing kids like me who spoke less-familiar languages. I also internalized the global historical bias against people of color that told even those of us living in diverse LA, and even those who spoke Spanish, that dark skin was worse than light skin. My first "bestie," Naomi, whose parents were both Black, had a deep carob complexion. Mine was a rich nut brown. On the playground, she and I were always forced to play "Indians" or "Robbers" or whatever bad-guy characters were in the mix. And if there was one worse option of toys or snacks shared among our friends, it always fell to Naomi, the darkest of us all.

Naomi's family moved to the Bahamas when we entered kindergarten in the 1980s. I continued to suffer while our peers branded me as strange and wrong. White boys in my kindergarten class taunted me every day for being Southeast Asian and mixed. I internalized the shame of this rejection and tried to distance myself from my mom. As harmful and painful as it was, their bullying made sense to me. I saw myself through a devastating lens of immutable inferiority. I believed I deserved to be treated poorly because of my race.

In elementary school, the bullying intensified, and I began to form a clear sense of what race meant from what my teachers, afterschool caregivers, and other students were saying and, in a more subliminal way, from what I was seeing on TV and in my community. I learned that you were born into a race, and it was in your blood. You inherited your race from your parents, who acquired it from theirs. There was no way of escaping it. It was intrinsically real.

I also gleaned that race required constant performance. I understood that different races were supposed to talk a certain way, act a certain way, and be destined for a certain kind of future. Your race determined your friends, your neighborhood, the kind of jobs your parents worked and how much money they had. You had to do your best within those constraints.

Mixed kids like me faced another layer of intricacy and confusion. My teachers and school administrators, who were mandated to pick one race for me, classified me as Pacific Islander. My mom and dad followed suit when they had to mark my race at the doctor's office or when filling out school forms. My peers, on the other hand, classified me as Asian; my close friends saw me as just mixed.

I donned various racial roles for different performances depending on the audience and venue. In the classroom, I marked the Pacific Islander box on my standardized tests, but on the playground, in the presence of fellow dark-skinned friends, I shifted to a more general "person of color" role. I constantly toggled between my official racial category as an Asian or Pacific Islander and my more intimate and informal mixed persona.

I also found myself switching between insider and outsider status within the various racial groups. Sure, I was "Brown," but I was still somewhat alien to most of my other Brown friends who were not mixed or who had a Latinx background. And I was most certainly alien to the East Asians, South Asians, and Ashkenazi Jewish kids in school. I was forced to embody a liminal position wherein I caught glimpses of what racialization was like for people of different races. I saw that negative characteristics were attributed to people who had dark skin no matter whether they were considered Black, like Naomi, or Pacific Islander or Asian, like my Indonesian kin. However, to "Black" were attributed the most negative characteristics of any race, and in a way it seemed these characteristics were inborn and could not change. Even my light-skinned peers who were mixed, with one Black parent and one White, were considered Black and stereotyped this way. My light-skinned Asian American and Latinx peers, who were attributed negative characteristics due to their racial identity, such as being untrustworthy, were seen as having the potential to acculturate and do well in school. Likewise, my Ashkenazi Jewish peers, despite also being painted negatively, were nonetheless assumed to have the potential to be smart and successful.

Not until I entered high school in the Coachella Valley in the 1990s did I find a friend who was going through a similar experience. My friend Kaiya was Black and Arab, with a skin tone and blended appearance similar to mine. At first we tried to be as agreeable as possible, to kill the "haters" with kindness by being congenial when we experienced a racial slight, to be the "bigger person." We tried to let microaggressive comments slide until finally they became overwhelming. But so many people stereotyped us and acted out their prejudices that we grew fed up.

However, even as we began speaking up to our fellow classmates, calling out racist epithets or stereotyped comments when we heard them, we realized that the issue extended beyond our fellow students, to our educators as well.

As a Black student, Kaiya was often a target of racist stereotypes. Despite being one of the highest-performing students in our grade, she was often shamed by an English teacher who went so far as to recommend she be removed from the class, taken off the AP English track, and put into a Remedial English class.

I would like to think that my schools were outliers, but they were not. I grew up in extremely diverse and relatively liberal communities in California where there was the potential for great awareness of the travails of racism. Still, whether I was in LA or the Coachella Valley, skinheads and White Nationalists were everywhere. At parties where I sought out the latest indie music, I moshed along with neo-

Nazis in their uniform of suspenders and steel-toed black boots with red and white shoelaces. But just because I chose to mosh with skinheads didn't mean I felt safe. When my neighbors or friends took me along to hang out with people I didn't know, I kept quiet if I was the only person of color.

In my last year of high school, at seventeen, as I repeatedly shapeshifted to adapt to different situations, I got an inkling of the complexity of my racial identity. I began to see myself from a distance, to intuit when I was playing a specific role such as nonthreatening light-skinned girl hanging in the shadows or bold Brown girl battling racial epithets. I also began to see how others played the hands they were dealt—people like my White friend Daniel who had let some older kid tattoo "White Power" across his belly with a homemade tattoo gun when he was in middle school. Daniel too would go from the shadows to the light as he concealed his identity from his peers of color only to reemerge donning his White Pride persona when in the company of other White supremacist teens. Kaiya and I talked about this code-switching and commiserated about how tiring it was to live what felt to us like multiple personalities. We shared how frustrated we were by feeling trapped to perform this way. Sometimes it seemed that only we were aware of how everyone was constantly performing their racial identity.

Kaiya and I couldn't wait to leave town and go to college somewhere more enlightened. We both applied to schools in Northern California and were elated when we both got into the University of California, Santa Cruz (UCSC). There, our first class was a freshman seminar in Race, Class, and Gender. Finally, we had arrived at a place where people were invested in racial justice and where we could explore race critically.

When we arrived at UCSC in the late 1990s, new thinking had recently come to light in the wider academic community: race had no basis in genetics. This idea was different from what we had been told as kids. We weren't "Asian" or "Black" because of inherited genetic traits from our parents. No DNA test could prove that a person was "Asian." In fact, race wasn't a biological concept at all but a social invention used to classify and separate groups of humans. Yet racial designation was no innocent mistake. It was a set of lies that Whites had invented long ago to justify enslavement and genocide: it was a fiction that literally killed.

We learned from our professors that race was a fiction, and as we looked into the new millennium, this set of ideas appeared in the media as well: by the late 1990s, magazines and newspapers like *The Atlantic* and *The New York Times* had begun reporting in depth on multiracial Americans like us. Journalists were drawing attention to our unstable experiences of race, racism, and identity. They were challenging the so-called reality of race as something fixed and unchanging, biological, built into our DNA code. Social scientists now viewed race as a social construct, a shifting, evolving thing invented by people in particular times and places, built into our social order.

By the time I left college, the leaders of the Human Genome Project—an international project attempting to identify, map, and sequence every gene in the human genome—revealed that the global mapping of the human genome proved humans were 99.9 percent the same. Broadcasting to nearly two dozen member-nations who had sponsored the Human Genome Project, President Bill Clinton publicized this statistic in a June 2000 speech at the White House ceremony commemorating the first publication of the map. With this data and the new insights from social science that race was a concept created by human interaction, the explanation "race is a social construct" became a useful catchphrase for those seeking to differentiate race and DNA. Together, geneticists and political leaders chanted a new mantra that there was no such thing as genetic race. They stood with countless other biologists, anthropologists, sociologists, psychologists, historians, and philosophers to proclaim race's nonbiological nature.

But as world leaders embraced the message, a new kind of confusion arose for me, Kaiya, and everyone who experienced race and racism as everyday realities. What did it mean to see race as social and not genetic? Reports often made it seem that if race was constructed, then it was make-believe and couldn't have real impacts. Was a social construct a bad or a good thing? Sometimes the phrase was used in a negative way, claiming that race was a deadly fiction determining the different ways we are treated in society. But our teachers had told us our race and culture were positive and should be embraced as an essential part of our identities and relationships that deserved to be celebrated. And most importantly, if race was not genetic, what was real about race?

BY THE TIME I decided to focus my career on the sociology of race, as I was commencing my graduate education in New York City in the early 2000s, the claim that "race is a social construct" had become an axiom so well supported as to be almost a cliché in scholarly circles. A generation of social scientists and humanists had amassed thousands of studies proving that racial categories and identities were fluid. These researchers found that racial classifications and their meanings changed over time, as did people's own racial self-conceptions and identities.

Meanwhile, anthropologists and biologists formally overturned the theory that race was genetic by conducting even more global genome-mapping projects that showed how genetically similar our species is and that all humans evolved from a single common ancestor somewhere in Africa. Contrary to the myth of a single Black "race," the African continent, where all humans first evolved, is home to more genetic diversity than anywhere else on Earth. According to the scientists mapping our shared origins, the concept of race was undoubtedly a manufactured fantasy.

Yet as new genome projects with innovative mapping technologies got underway, a debate erupted about whether there was something real about race that scientists might have missed. Leading genomic scientists in the wake of the Human Genome Project struggled to create a new concept of race devoid of "genetic determinism"—the misconception that genes simply rule human behavior—yet one that acknowledged that there were meaningful differences between different groups. From nearly a decade of research I conducted into genome mapping, I found that many of the leaders of the major international gene-mapping efforts had deeply personal stakes in shaping public thought around race. They were concerned about battling racism, and most hoped that their work would dispel the conviction that our DNA programmed our race. However, many of these same project leaders were inadvertently reinforcing a genetic idea of race. Their efforts had not disentangled race from DNA as they had hoped.

As I worked at Brown University, in the Division of Biology and Medicine, the Department of Africana Studies, and Science and Technology Studies, and then at the University of California, San Francisco (UCSF), one of the world's top universities in clinical medicine, I began teaching about racial identity and myths about the relationship between genetics and race. I encountered misconceptions among my first-year students and also in people at the top of their fields in technology, medicine, and genetics. Even some of the leading geneticists training the next generation of physicians and health scientists at our medical schools told me how confused they were about what was true and what was false about race.

At the National Institutes of Health Center for Transdisciplinary Ethical, Legal, and Social Implications (ELSI) Research in Translational Genomics—a genomic research institute housed at UCSF's Institute for Human Genetics—I spearheaded a working group of experts dedicated to eradicating genetic determinism around race, gender, and ethnicity. At the same time, I launched a study of genetic trends within different kinds of social behavior, such as rape, gang membership, and violent behavior. I found that many of the gene-mapping efforts in the space of social behavior arose from partnerships between social and genetic science. In many cases, social scientists, even social scientists of race like me, were leading genetic research. I wondered if these sociologically minded studies would do a better job of differentiating race and DNA.

I found that much of the genetics of social behavior—what genomic scientist Gene Robinson coined "sociogenomics" in the early 2000s—was conflating race and DNA just as mainstream genomic science had. US population projections had just determined that America would become a "minority majority" nation in 2044, with people of color making up over 51 percent of the population. Genome scientists were scrambling to include more racial minorities in their research. It was now commonplace to see headlines about genes for this or that disease (heart disease, hypertension, cancer, etc.) or behavior (aggressiveness, promiscuity, criminality, etc.) reported in terms of a person's race.

Looking closely at the sociogenomic research community, I found that, like mainstream genome mappers, leaders of sociogenomic studies hoped their research would dispel genetic determinism, especially around race. Yet the DNA collections, databases, and algorithms with which they worked were stratified by race. Scientists were inadvertently paving the way for racial comparisons of traits like intelligence and criminality. Suddenly, genetic notions of race were again on the rise.

I moved to Rutgers University in 2020 to further expand my investigations in the emerging science of genome editing—what many refer to as "CRISPR" science and technology.* Working with scientists like Jennifer Doudna, Emmanuelle Charpentier, and George Church, I found that the field's leading developers were deeply concerned about the potential for racist misuses of their science. At the same time, many gene-editing companies were intensifying their analysis of the relationship between genes and cognition, and some DNA test makers who linked race to a fixed genetic notion of intelligence were offering DNA IQ tests to the public. There were even biotech firms exploring ways to use racially stratified genomic data to boost cognition and select embryos for higher intelligence. In 2021, the biotech firm Bio-Viva injected six patients with genes edited to rejuvenate their brain cells. The race for superhuman brainpower was on.

I determined to expose this unfolding enterprise as well as the racist history of intelligence genetics that these innovations were built

---

* Gene editing is a method of making changes to a genome. Presently, CRISPR, which stands for "clustered regularly interspaced short palindromic repeats," is the primary technology that scientists use to make edits.

on. Reviewing centuries of genetic research and development, and the racism that intelligence genetics had spawned, made it clear that any claim that your intelligence is tied to some genetic marker or indicator only perpetuates the body of racial stereotypes that afflict our world. From this research, I concluded that instead of seeing intelligence as programmed by our DNA and using risky gene-editing technologies to boost the brain, we must see intelligence as a social process of learning from our environments. Human intelligence is an emergent, creative process that all people engage in no matter who they are and what their race is.

My research over these past decades has made it evident to me that we still need a deeper understanding of the fluid nature of genetics and race. In recent years, genetic and social researchers have ramped up their analyses into the undeniably real effects of race. Yet, the new technologies that we are creating are perpetuating old systems of harm, in particular old systems of racism, in new ways. From genomic science, we know that race may not be genetically "real," yet we experience it as a mundane fact of life, spinning in the background, constantly shaping us in unseen ways. From social science, we know that race is also deeply politicized—it conditions our ability to access rights and resources—and yet we don't get to choose our race, because how others see us is something physiological that we cannot control.

Race matters. It doesn't matter. Race is real. It's a lie.

With each new scientific advance, we have had a fresh opportunity to redefine race and rid our beliefs of genetic determinism. Yet, confusion reigns. This book stems from a desire to use my unique expertise as a scholar of genetics and society to answer thorny questions like: How did the categories of race emerge and how did they get embedded in modern-day science? How are scientists misusing DNA collections and genetic research that are stratified by race? Are there ethical ways to consider and study race in science? And the burning question that many of us continue to ask ourselves: If race is a social construct, then what's real about race?

BEFORE I BEGIN TO address those puzzles, I want to unpack the sentence "race is a social construct." When we say "race is a social construct," what do we really mean?

Let's look at it sociologically. Saying something is "social" means that the phenomenon in question exists because of and for people. It is forged through our membership and belonging in society. It is a phenomenon that is experienced in human-level interactions and connections, such as the all too real bullying and shaming that Kaiya and I experienced in school.

Saying something is "constructed" means that the phenomenon exists because people together have made it real. When something is made from human collaboration, it is malleable, built on and constantly shaped by the ever-changing body of ideas that people share. But a construct's malleability makes it no less real. Kaiya and I were locked in collaboration with the very people with whom we disagreed as we struggled to remake this thing that had shaped our life experiences. Kaiya, my classmates, and I used our real shared experiences to put our own spin on the meaning of racial differences in ways that we believed could serve us better.

In fact, calling race (or anything) a "social construct" is simultaneously redundant and contradictory. Anything constructed, or invented, only exists because of its social nature—real people have worked together, socially, to make it real. And yet invented constructs are inherently real and not fake—a phenomenon like race exists because we agree that it does and then we construct our reality around it.

These unseen redundancies and contradictions are what make social constructs feel so unsettling and unreal when we ponder them. Birthdays, for example, are social constructs, and because they're so entrenched in our culture, it's strange to think of them as an invention. After all, we experience them in real social interactions—our celebrations—and the meaning that they give to our lives is real. However, birthdays are celebrated differently in different cultures, and have been celebrated differently by the same cultures in different times— they are real *and* constructed. Those variations in the same custom over time and place don't make your very real version of a birthday untrue, because social constructs are the building blocks of social reality. Our world is based on the meaning we breathe into it.

Politicized constructs like race are even stranger to reflect on because they impact our deepest thoughts and emotions without us necessarily being aware. We make race real through a vast web of tangible and intangible experiences, from differences in skin color and hair texture that we see in the individuals we interact with every day, to political struggles over police violence and racism in schools. Even if we are not passionate about race relations, as Kaiya and I grew to be, we are aware of how others identify us racially—Black, White, Asian, Latinx, Indigenous, or otherwise—and what those terms and categories can realistically mean. If you were born into a different society, your concept of race might be different. Yet the fact that race means different things in different societies doesn't negate the meaning that you attribute to race in your life.

Consider it from a linguistic perspective. We have language for real things, like the word "table" for a flat surface held up by legs, but the word itself is symbolic, even though the object is real. The word is a symbol we agree to use to reference something. When we move to another culture or setting (or as Kaiya and I learned as we code-switched in our performances from environments where we felt safe to speak out against racism to ones in which we felt we had to keep silent), we often must find a new way of referencing the object in order to express ourselves.

In the same way, racialized characteristics like skin color, eye shape, and hair texture reference real bodies of real people—people like Kaiya and me and our light-skinned antagonists—even though the categories themselves are not real. Racial categories are symbols that function like conceptual eyeglasses. When we see through the lens of these constructed racial categories, we notice real things like skin color, eye shape, and hair texture, and we attribute meaning to those differences.

Bizarrely, a person might be considered a completely different race in one country than in another. In Indonesia, where most of my relatives live, people attach a completely different set of physiological reference points to categories of race. While in the United States we obsess over White, Black, Asian, American Indian, Pacific Islander, and Latinx distinctions, in Indonesia a primary concern is distinguishing East Asian from Malay (people originating in China, Korea, Hong Kong, Japan, Macau, and Taiwan versus people indigenous to Indonesia, Malaysia, and Brunei). Moreover, Indonesians link the dominant religion of Islam with Malay, while we in the United States see Islam as Arab (not Asian). As a result, the features Americans observe most closely, such as facial features, are less important in Indonesia. There, hair color and texture are practically irrelevant for making everyday distinctions. And because light skin color is valued at a premium, Indonesians hold more nuanced categories of racial classification based on color. People literally see and construct the world around them differently, and as a result I am viewed differently in the two countries.

The subtle differences in how we look are real and unchangeable, but we construct different meanings on top of them. We see race, make decisions about ourselves and others, and relate to people based on our biases. We take physical things, like bodies, and overlay constructed (invented) meanings on them only to build a new reality out of those meanings.

So, race is not just a lie. And it's not only a fiction. It is reality too.

RACE IS A FICTION—a relatively recent concept in human history that has changed shape and form many times in the hands of a wide variety of thinkers. Yet this fiction has also created real social consequences and experiences.

Beyond being a social construct, race is a social *reality*, with huge impacts on our life chances, class, and health. There's nothing biological or scientific about race, yet it is continually made reality, first by how we interpret and experience our bodies and our feelings, and how those interpretations affect our life chances. It is further made reality in the ways that racial discrimination endangers people and society.

Science springs from our intrinsic desire to know ourselves and to understand our place in the world, and science has the potential to clarify race's materiality. Yet science is not foolproof. The misconception that there is a genetic basis for race arose from a host of scientific lies perpetrated over centuries, most willfully conducted to shore up support for racist politics. Given this history, we must take a close look at how scientists have used and continue to use racial categories. We must unpack how labels of race are mobilized and materialized, and to what ends.

Our uncertainty about race stems from its immateriality. Race started as an idea based on unscientific guesses about biology. But over a long history of confusing genetic differences with racial differences and structuring our society based on these flawed racial categories, race has become reality. It is built into our everyday lives. It determines how we think of ourselves and others, and how we treat people and are treated. Our race can impact what schools we get into, the jobs we get, what fields we work in, where we live, whom we partner with, whom we marry and make family with. And as is evident in world politics, where we are safe.

So, when we characterize race, we must proclaim its "social reality" and make this the object of our analysis, both in scientific and critical pursuits. With this new characterization of race, we may reconstruct race to render a more accurate and humane reality.

CHAPTER 1

A Brief History of Race

A S MEANINGFUL AS RACE MAY seem today, humans have not always lived with the concept. The idea of race was created as a way to interpret and manage the diversity of humanity. Naturalists in seventeenth- and eighteenth-century Europe invented the idea of race to sort through the flood of data returning with explorers and colonists traveling the globe. Tales of barbaric people in far-off lands and strange civilizations inspired them to carve humanity into color-coded continental varieties (literally: Black, White, Yellow, Red). Monarchs and fledgling republics adopted these categories to rationalize enslavement, forced labor, and colonization, and to administer their territories at home and abroad.

Before there was race, there was nativism—the belief that native-born people are distinct from foreign-born people—and native-born supremacy—the belief that native-born people are inherently better than foreign-born people. However, nativism was never imagined on a global scale. Instead, ancient Egyptians pitted themselves against their neighbors the Nubians, while ancient Greeks pitted themselves against *their* neighbors the ancient Egyptians. Romans depicted themselves as unique and distinct from every culture they encountered in Eurasia and Africa. The ancient Chinese who lived in the vicinity of their emperors set themselves apart from other tribes and cultures that inhabited wider Eurasia. Ancient cultures distinguished between native and foreign populations, and some relied on these distinctions to wage war, enslavement, and genocide on others, but they did not view different continents as having their own unique traits.

In these early human civilizations, the feature that made native-born people special was ill-defined, but it was generally assumed to run along bloodlines. Indigenous Americans and nomadic peoples, for example, considered those who were born into a tribal community to be tribal members. Blood inheritance was more important than the geographical location in which an individual was born and was never seen in terms of a continental origin as race later came to signify, as evident, for example, in the many wars and genocidal campaigns executed in the Iberian Peninsula or British Isles before and after the Romans invaded their territories in 218 BCE and 43 AD, respectively. Inhabitants born in these places but of a distinct bloodline (i.e., what we today would refer to as "Scottish," "Jewish," or "Moorish") were victimized regardless of having spent their whole lives on what was deemed native ground. Generations of living in a specific territory could do nothing to erase the label of outsiderness based on one's ancestry.

Obsession with bloodlines was also evident in the terminology that the ancients used to distinguish foreign residents—for example, the *metics* of ancient Greece. Until the fall of the Greek peninsula to the Romans in 146 BC, through Roman rule in the first century AD, immigrants or descendants of immigrants living in Athens were often culturally, economically, and physiologically indistinguishable from citizens, yet they carried the label *metic* and were prohibited from holding political office.

Many ancient civilizations also held a binary sense of nativist superiority: they believed that nearly all who lived outside of their city walls were animal-like barbarians. In fact, "barbarian" comes from the Greek *bárbaros*, or "babbler," because the Greeks saw foreign speakers as blathering aliens. The ancient Chinese similarly called anyone living outside the walled zones of China *huang fu*, or "barbarians of the wild zone." Those deemed *huang fu* were considered untamed, uncivilized, and deadly.

Prior to rapid transportation and globalization, it was difficult to travel far enough to see people who had radically different cultures and appearances. For this reason, leaders emphasized minor cultural differences to draw distinctions. Neighbors who looked alike but sounded or dressed differently were often characterized as uncouth and painted as lethal enemies. Romans, for example, called themselves the "togaed people" and made fun of their geographic neighbors the Gauls, who wore shirts and pants, but they lauded Ethiopians who wore regal gowns. In this case, inferiority was not a matter of skin color, but rather of customs and civility.

Not until the time of Marco Polo did Europeans begin to have widespread awareness of other continents on which foreign people lived—people whom they would begin to describe, in the seventeenth century, as being of different races. During the Scientific Revolution and the Renaissance, cartographers began to report the true contours of the Earth to their European royal benefactors. Like ancient guesses about foreigners, these projections of world geography ranged from semi-informed to highly inaccurate. It was then that "human kinds," a crude theory that roughly corresponds to what we know as "race," emerged from an unlikely source.

IN 1665, FRANÇOIS BERNIER left his home in Paris to travel to the far-off continents of Asia and Africa. When he embarked on his journey, he had almost no scientific training, yet his writings on race would become an essential framework to understand human difference for centuries to come. Bernier was the first to use the term "race" to describe the people of different continents.

How did a traveling secretary have the authority to write about such matters? After taking a three-month medical course, Bernier was licensed as a physician on the condition that he would never practice medicine inside France. Based on his assessments of people he had met and treated in the Middle East and Northern Africa, and other travelers' portrayals of people from Asia and the Americas, he used his limited anatomical understanding to write "The New Division of Earth by the Different Species or Races Which Inhabit It." This essay, which he managed to publish anonymously in Europe's then-premier academic journal, separated humans into four races: European, African, Asian, and Lapp (the group indigenous to Scandinavia and Russia with which Bernier was most familiar, now known as the Sámi).

Bernier marked a turn both from the nativism of ancient cultures and from the biblical notion of common descent among humans. He was not interested in regional differences in culture and politics, factors that were subsumed under his racial groupings. Rather, he was obsessed with broad physiological distinctions that he believed were inherited and distinct for each continental group because each had its own unique biology and lineage. For example, Bernier reported that Lapps were "ugly animals" with faces like bears. He believed that all Arctic peoples, no matter where in the Arctic they were born or how they lived, possessed these innate characteristics.

This first iteration of the concept of race—a system of distinct, rankable continental groups—established several conventions, many of which endure today despite the fact that Bernier wrote over 350 years ago. First, his essay established the convention of characterizing races as continental "species," mutually exclusive populations that arose separately and developed their own unique physiological characteristics (I call this "continental race"). Second, Bernier emphasized skin color as a defining factor and a visual indicator of a person's true race, a practice that continues even now. Third, the report held Europeans as the supreme race, with only negative characteristics attributed to all others. Fourth, it established the convention of characterizing European features as ideal and divine and all others as profane and animalistic, or inhuman.

Bernier was welcomed into the major literary salons of Paris and London, where his ideas grew popular among Europe's literati. His writings also became a foundation for other naturalists seeking to characterize the great "divisions of Earth" by humankind.

The next major definition of race emerged almost a century later, from the "father of taxonomy," Carl von Linné, or Linnaeus. Like Bernier, Linnaeus conceived of his classification system while on an expedition undertaken shortly after finishing a brief medical apprenticeship. After completing a two-week doctorate in medicine at the University of Harderwijk in 1735, the Swedish naturalist published a human taxonomy of four races as part of his broader biological taxonomy in a work entitled *Systema Naturae*. Yet since a great deal more had by then been written on indigenous Americans, in place of Lapps Linnaeus listed "Americans" alongside the continental groupings of Asian, African, and European.

But the most original dimension of his version compared to Bernier's was the inclusion of social and behavioral characteristics, which he characterized as inborn traits exclusive to each race. *Homo Americanus* was "red," "unyielding," "cheerful," and "free." *Homo Asiaticus* was "sallow," "stern," "haughty," and "greedy." *Homo Afer* was "black," "sly," "sluggish," and "neglectful." But *Homo Europaeus* was "white," "light," "wise," and a born "inventor." This convention of coupling physical and mental traits and attributing nearly all positive behavioral qualities to Europeans and all negative to other races became a mainstay of the social construction of race.

Subsequent naturalists of the late-eighteenth-century Enlightenment presented new iterations of race. Georges-Louis Leclerc (the Comte de Buffon) and Johannes Blumenbach recognized Bernier's and Linnaeus's races as variations of one human species. They posited that Europeans were the first humans and that all other races had degenerated as they had moved from Europe to other continents. They further considered the other races to be in dire need of European civilization. Leclerc argued, for example, that Indigenous Americans' supposedly inborn drive to be savage necessitated European imperialist mastery. Blumenbach—whose taxonomy of Caucasian, Mongolian, Malayan, Ethiopian, and American corresponds to the current categories of White, Asian, Pacific Islander, Black, and Native American used by the US government as well as most biomedical and public health organizations—agreed that the degenerate bodies and minds of the various races outside of Europe demanded the fairer, smarter Europeans to domesticate them.

Still other naturalists and philosophers working in the late eighteenth century, including those focused on theorizing morality and ethics, wrote that only Europeans could improve themselves. These scholars maintained that there was no hope for the betterment of degenerate races, even those living in modern, so-called civilized circumstances. David Hume, for example, argued that only Europeans were born to reason. Africans had no possibility of learning, and therefore were biologically destined for slavery. Immanuel Kant echoed that only the "inborn seeds" of European bloodlines conferred the capacity to reason, to have intelligence, and to be moral. Georges Cuvier, the "father of paleontology," claimed that Africans had degenerated so far from Adam and Eve as to be indistinguishable from apes. Though Hume never left Europe, Cuvier never left France, and Kant spent his entire life in his German hometown of Königsberg, their theories about the innate inferiority of non-Europeans had considerable influence across Europe and the colonial world. Untested by any real experience with "degenerate" populations on their part, their ideas infused all the sciences emerging from the Enlightenment, from biology to psychology to politics.

From Bernier's early Enlightenment–era continental iteration of race to Kant's late-Enlightenment moral and philosophical iteration, scholars enriched the theories that preceded their own, building a cohesive paradigm that we may call "Enlightenment Race." It characterized the Earth as comprising four or five continental races with mutually distinct traits and capacities, all destined to be ruled by the European race. Because Enlightenment theorists faced no burden of proof, as later scientists would, and thus were free to deduce their theories of race from the comfort of their homes, the theory of Enlightenment Race they devised insidiously spread, subsuming preexisting nativist beliefs while promoting popular new understandings of species. Enlightenment Race rapidly infiltrated European politics and culture based on its ability to corroborate a deepening supremacy that enabled colonization, enslavement, and genocide.

THE NEXT MAJOR ITERATION of race came in the early 1800s, with the revolutionary work of Charles Darwin. Darwin was part of a new, modern era of science marked by inductive reasoning in which scholars observed and interacted with the world around them to identify patterns and trends. With this new emphasis on collecting original data, Darwin was unique, compared to the many Enlightenment philosophers who came before him, in traveling to meet some of the peoples living outside Europe about whom he wrote. From firsthand analysis of biological evidence that he collected, Darwin theorized that all creatures on the planet were related by intracellular units of heredity that were passed on from generation to generation. His research substantiated the late-Enlightenment supposition that there were five continental subspecies, all descended from a common ancestor.

Darwin's iteration of race was different from previous ones because he characterized races as being equally fit to survive. In his groundbreaking work, *On the Origin of Species by Means of Natural Selection, Or the Preservation of Favoured Races in the Struggle for Life* (1859), Darwin argued that though evolution was a matter of a struggle for existence, humans of all ilk persevered and were successful. In addition, no matter what they looked like on the outside, all humans could procreate with one another, the defining characteristic of a species. According to Darwin, no biological principle prevented races from mixing.

However, Darwin's concept of race adhered to previous iterations because he too ranked the races, placing Europeans on top. Although he deeply disfavored slavery, in his second masterwork, *The Descent of Man, and Selection in Relation to Sex* (1871), Darwin portrayed Africans as evolutionarily situated between Europeans and apes. Ultimately, he came to support the likes of Hume, Kant, and Cuvier in claiming that human subspecies, or "races," did really exist, and only the European race was capable of intelligence. In fact, Darwin echoed Cuvier in saying that "Negro" skulls were more akin to those of apes. He also argued for controlled breeding—what would come to be known as "eugenics"—and contended that letting the "weak . . . propagate their kind" would cause the human species to degenerate.

Darwin inspired his cousin, fellow evolutionist Francis Galton, to pen his own more aggressively supremacist definition of race. Born into a genteel British family of inventors, entrepreneurs, and scientists, Galton developed the first full-scale research program into human racial difference at his laboratories in London. He characterized races in terms of Darwin's five subspecies and insisted on the intellectual fitness and supremacy of upper-class Europeans and the general fitness and supremacy of Europeans over all other continental races. Galton's inclusion of class in definitions of racial fitness gave race new meaning. He also came up with a unique theory of race, claiming that selective breeding was a requirement for the survival of humanity because inferior populations bred faster than superior ones. To collect data to support this genetic notion of White supremacy, and to outfit his selective breeding campaigns with a theory of "better breeding," Galton developed his own science of measurement, giving way to statistics and the medical case history that healthcare providers, physicians, and scientists use today. He coined the term "eugenics" and embarked upon a political campaign to instate racial breeding and extermination.

Darwinian evolution and Galton's eugenics movement engendered

a new paradigm of race that I call "Modern Race." Like Enlightenment Race, Modern Race saw humanity divided by continental origin,
with Europeans dominating other races. However, Modern Race went
a step further, explicitly linking perceived biological and intellectual
disparities between people originating from different continents to a
difference in genetics. Indoctrinating racism with scientific thinking,
this belief in *genetic* superiority justified theories of White supremacy
and eugenics: Modern Race explicitly focused on gaming the genetic
fitness of the human species by directing certain populations to breed
and pass on their genetic heritage, while eliminating others from existence by any means necessary.

Modern Race was initially controversial. Theories of evolution
went against dominant religious beliefs, such as the notion that God
had created ancestral divergences from the lineage of Adam and Eve.
Many scientists developed alternative ways of measuring and justifying
White supremacy so that they could square their theories about race
and ancestry with Christian doctrine. A cadre of scholars argued for
"polygeny," the view that only Whites descended from Adam and Eve,
and that races must never mix their gene pools. Geologist Louis Agassiz, Egyptologist George Gliddon, physicians Josiah Nott and Samuel
Morton, and others drew on a combination of geographical, cultural,
and "biblical" history to argue that humans did not come from the
same stock, and that races were altogether separate animals. However,
the growing popularity of evidence-based science, and the establishment of biology as a discipline in the eighteenth century, propelled
Modern Race forward to become the dominant worldview.

The colonies in America, and the US republic that followed from
them, are an interesting case in point. The first census, taken in 1790,
recognized "free White females and males," "other free persons," and

"slaves." Yet as the idea of Darwinian evolution spread, these classifications grew more explicit and nuanced as censuses went from counting only Black/Mulattoes and Whites to adding Chinese and American Indians to the roster.* This four-continent classification system— White, Black, Chinese, Indian— reflected the taxonomies popularized by anthropologists, biologists, and medical experts of the time who were disseminating Darwinian and Galtonian genetic science to Europe, its colonies, and the Americas.

As states in the United States adopted the Modern Race continental taxonomy throughout the latter half of the nineteenth century, lawmakers devised eugenic policies and sanctions against interracial relationships. Many states also developed a system of blood quantum measurement that assigned people with at least one non-European ancestor to the race of that ancestor (what policymakers and analysts came to call the "one-drop rule") unless they held land rights that behooved states to classify them as White. Most people with at least one known Black ancestor were therefore considered Black. Most children born to a White parent and a Native American parent were considered Native American. The coexistence of blood quantum policy and the one-drop rule maximized states' access to labor while minimizing people's individual claims to territory based on ancestry.

The federal government also implemented Modern Race classification in education and immigration policy. Throughout the late 1800s, doctors, scientists, and educators worked tirelessly to characterize and assess human intelligence in racial and ethnic groups. Internationally

---

* In other parts of colonial America, such as the former French and Spanish colonies of Louisiana and Florida, racial classification systems were even more complex, including more subdivisions in racial categories.

acclaimed works on the genetics of intelligence such as Galton's *Hereditary Genius* (1869) and medical tracts such as John Langdon Down's "Observations on the Ethnic Classification of Idiots" (1866) motivated experts and officials to view intelligence in terms of a bell curve, with northwestern Europeans at the "genius" end of the scale and Asians and Africans at the "imbecile" end.

Down, for example, whose name we know in reference to "Down syndrome," or trisomy 21, argued that Europeans with that trait had genetically reverted to a "Mongolian" racial type. Down named the disease "Mongolian Imbecility" and proceeded to create a full-scale racial "classification of idiots" that likened Asians and Africans to "simians." Galton agreed and warned that the European race would degenerate if mixed with other racial stock. He envisioned a genocide of the weakest races and redistribution of land among the superior races. To prevent degeneration of the human species, he called for segregation keeping races to their own continents.

Amid such warnings by the most prominent scientists of the age, the US government instituted the country's first race-based exclusion act: the Chinese Exclusion Act of 1882. Down's language of "idiocy" dovetailed with political pressure from White laborers who blamed Chinese immigrants for their economic troubles, inspiring federal policymakers to make the case that Asians were a peril to White America. The Chinese Exclusion Act barred Chinese migrants from American soil and was eventually broadened to exclude all people from Asia as well as other groups, such as Africans, deemed to be racially unfit.

The turn of the twentieth century was an important time for the science of race. It was also a critical moment for the burgeoning field of genetics, which emerged through the measurement of racial differences as researchers compared skull sizes and genitalia, performed statistical regressions of intelligence, plotted bell curves of racial vigor, and concocted damning lineages to justify slavery, colonization, sterilization, and extermination of anyone classified other than European.

Many of the men who pursued the new science of genetics and popularized Modern Race in the first decades of the twentieth century were socially and politically progressive. Most of them had opposed the idea of slavery, and many believed that races could coexist peacefully. In *The Mind of Primitive Man* (1911), for example, anthropologist Franz Boas argued that there were no significant differences in mental or physical fitness between races, and that cultural and environmental factors determined human development. Still, Boas believed that races existed. He did not challenge the reigning taxonomy nor the notion of biological races. Consequently, even some of his followers supported some form of eugenics.

The beginning of the century witnessed the establishment of myriad new eugenics societies and eugenic political campaigns. From the Eugenics Education Society in Britain to the German Society for Racial Hygiene and the Race Betterment Foundation in the United States, these scientific brotherhoods traded in the latest racial studies in hopes that they could improve their countries' bloodlines. Their goal was not just to proliferate the so-called "good" genetic lineages but also to terminate the "bad" ones. In eugenics, genetics, race science, politics, and governance became one.

In 1912, the world's first International Conference of Eugenics was held in London. The conference was presided over by Major Leonard Darwin, an intelligence operative, former member of parliament, and Charles Darwin's son. Hundreds gathered to discuss the implementation of their race science in foreign and domestic policy. Winston Churchill parleyed with the founders of the American Genetics Association, while Major Darwin, then chair of the British Eugenics Society and president of the Royal Geographical Society, talked geopolitics with Chief Justice Arthur Balfour to construct a cohesive statement on the reality of race and a tailored form of governance and society.

For the next meeting, held in 1921 at the American Museum of Natural History in New York, the US State Department sent invitations to leaders around the world. At the time, eugenics was seen as the pinnacle of human progress and genocide a necessary strategy to achieve human perfection. Eugenics had infiltrated governance and was a national priority for countries worldwide. Legislators toiled over implementation in their states and provinces. What historians now refer to as "positive eugenics," or policies to encourage "good" stock to breed, were being eclipsed by "negative eugenics," policies of sterilization, internment, incarceration, and extermination.

The categories that counted as races changed over time and were often mobilized in contradictory ways during the same historical moment, but the Modern Race notion of continental genetic subspecies held fast. For example, members of the dominant European settler-colonial lineages in the United States, such as Anglo-Americans, concocted taxonomies to shore up xenophobia against specific groups (e.g., the Irish, Italians, and Eastern Europeans). Meanwhile, those same settler-colonialists defined "White" as an exclusive club that people had to formally or informally petition to join. Ultimately, by law, your race and not your country of origin determined your citizenship, and full citizenship was reserved for Whites of European origin. For example, when Bhagat Singh Thind, a decorated soldier in the US Army who hailed from India, petitioned the federal government for naturalization as an Aryan member of the White race in 1923, the Supreme Court denied him citizenship on the grounds that ethnicities like

Aryan were linguistic and not genetic. Thind did not meet the "common sense" understanding of White, which was rooted in genetics as opposed to language.

As geneticists churned out new classifications and new continental comparisons, politicians mobilized their ideas to devastating ends. Later that year, the US government devised more racial bans on immigration, which were signed into effect with the Johnson-Reed Act of 1924. Adolf Hitler praised the US government for its efforts to control the racial makeup of the nation. In *Mein Kampf* (1925), he wrote that barring "unhealthy elements" and banning "the immigration of certain races" was the paragon of good governance, and he called the United States a beacon for all other governments. Both it and Germany soon instituted programs of forced sterilizations, incarceration, internment, and "mercy killings," with the United States arriving at a toll of approximately 65,000 sterilizations of people classified as "morons," "idiots," or "imbeciles," most often Black Americans and other people of color. Nazi Germany went to horrifying extremes, carrying out over ten million exterminations of those deemed unfit, such as Jews, Romani, Sinti, Jehovah's Witnesses, and gay, lesbian, and transgender people.

Eugenics remained popular with world leaders even into the beginning of World War II. Though we often think about the war as an effort by the United States, Great Britain, and the Soviet Union to save Jews from genocide, the allied powers did not oppose "racial hygiene." Even as the international news media reported on atrocities committed by the Nazis in the years leading up to the war, the United States took no action until Hitler began invading other countries and threatening their autonomy.

Popular sentiment remained aligned with the US government's

policy on immigration and sterilization throughout most of the war, and this meant that the allied powers showed widespread support for eugenics while fighting the Third Reich. When Americans and European allies were asked whether they supported Nazism, they answered "no." But when asked whether they supported rescue missions and intake of immigrants, they also answered "no."

Not until the final days of the war, when popular media began circulating photos of concentration camps, did public and scientific opinion change. After Hitler's defeat, as the Allies formed the United Nations (UN) and dedicated themselves to preventing war, and as Jewish refugees filtered into the United States, voices critical of totalitarianism and race science began to take center stage.

In the years after war's end in 1945, the UN issued the Universal Declaration of Human Rights and its first human rights treaty, the Genocide Convention, which explicitly banned wartime and peacetime harm of "a national, ethnical, racial or religious group." The UN also established UNESCO (United Nations Educational, Scientific, and Cultural Organization), a scholarly agency dedicated to advancing world peace, which wrote into its constitution a promise to put an end to "the doctrine of inequality of men and races." Leading scientists from around the world, some of whom were Jewish and African American, began drafting a series of statements on race that provided the latest in genetic and social science to advance that goal.

The new doctrine on race that UNESCO issued in the postwar period—what I call "UNESCO Race"—claimed that races were inherently equal. In a series of statements, UNESCO argued that racial bias was unscientific. Races had similar mental capacities and were equally fit. They did not degenerate by admixture.

While UNESCO's views on race diverged from Modern Race in

promoting the concept of racial equality, it still situated race as a biological fact. UNESCO's first statement, issued in 1950, was hazy on the actual definition of race. By inaccurately linking race and biology, UNESCO's first statement furthered the confusion about race in the postwar period.

Later statements, such as the second UNESCO statement, issued in 1951, included the participation of evolutionary biologists who had expertise about genetic inheritance. Their revised definition of race held that within a species, races were "groups of mankind possessing well-developed and primarily heritable physical differences from other groups." Race was a "zoological frame," a tool for analysis of "evolutionary processes." In this sense, the scientists drafting UNESCO's statement deemed race genetically and biologically real, akin to Darwin's own concept of race as genetic subspecies, and coincident with Enlightenment Race as continental varieties.

The conclusion of the UNESCO statements on race was that there were indeed races, and that those races were indeed biological entities. According to this, human races were the result of the evolutionary adaptation of our genes to varying continental environments. Yet though humans had diverged into separate races, all races were equally fit. The UNESCO statements maintained that there was no biological basis for White supremacy or for keeping races from breeding with each other. Anyone interested in understanding the origins of racial inequality would need to refer to history and social science, not biology and genetics. Anyone interested in ameliorating racial inequality would need to use social policy, not eugenic science, to improve the human condition.

THE END OF THE postwar period and the beginning of the civil rights era in the United States saw more atrocities committed in the name of eugenics. Yet, among scientists, medical experts, and laypeople, there was also a growing acceptance of the UNESCO conclusions, especially regarding the inaccuracy of prior convictions about innate racial inequality. People around the world were starting to accept the UN's definitions of race and genocide, and they were coming to acknowledge the systematic forms of racism that their governments were responsible for. In countries far and wide, advocacy groups and communities often pushed to desegregate social institutions like education, which had been segregated based on the faulty notion that Europeans were genetically superior and that races should never mix. The "true" biology of race as put forth by UNESCO Race—that races exist as equally fit genetic subspecies—became a truism for those working inside and outside scientific laboratories. As governments worked on new laws to instate the equality of all races, the question of whether distinct races exist biologically became less of a question and more of a commonly understood fact.

In 1961, President John F. Kennedy signed Executive Order 10925 into effect, a law that banned employer discrimination according to "race, creed, color, or national origin." He also proposed the Civil Rights Act that would desegregate all US institutions. Shortly following Kennedy's assassination, President Lyndon B. Johnson signed the act into effect and issued Executive Order 11246, promising to realize equal opportunity of employment through "a positive, continuing program in each executive department and agency" of the US federal government—what is now known as affirmative action. In 1965, President Johnson signed the Voting Rights Act and ratified the Hart-Celler Immigration and Naturalization Act, which repealed the race- and nation-based immigration acts of the Progressive Era and set America on course for equal treatment of foreign-born nationals. Fair Housing acts soon followed.

With the ratification of these new acts, the US government shifted away from negative rights that protected citizens from government harm toward positive rights that ensured that the government would provide equal access to public institutions. But to ensure these rights were put into effect, the federal government needed an official racial taxonomy to apply to populations to measure access. So, in 1974, the government convened a Committee on Racial and Ethnic Definitions from the very agencies responsible for racial and ethnic data collection and use. The committee delineated four races (White, Black, Asian/ Pacific Islander, American Indian/Alaska Native), which they warned "should not be interpreted as scientific." However, this committee said nothing about the actual meaning of race. As they mandated the use of race, giving it the imprimatur of officialdom, the Committee on Racial and Ethnic Definitions left it to users to make their own interpretations of the correspondence of race to genetics.

In its final edict, "Office of Management and Budget Directive No. 15," the committee gave further credence to the notion that races were original continental peoples. They classified "Hispanic" as a potential ethnicity and directed people who self-identified as such to be further tabulated as "White" or "Black." This committed Americans to adhering to the "one-drop rule," the idea that any blood inheritance of non-European ancestry made a person ineligible to be classified as a member of the White race. A person could only be one race, never more. This law forcing government officials, public administrators, public servants, and eventually all publicly funded institutions to categorize race in terms of continents made race out to be both social *and* biological. UNESCO Race, which was seen as progressive and liberatory for foregrounding the social reality of race—bias and racism—also reinscribed the idea of continental race. The institutionalization of UNESCO Race as discrete continental populations would create enormous problems in the decades to come.

CHAPTER 2

The Genomics of Race

I N THE FINAL DECADES OF the twentieth century, the Office of Management and Budget (OMB)—a vast office that oversees federal agencies and the census—identified the need for consistent racial and ethnic data across the federal government. In 1977, the OMB adopted Directive No. 15 ("OMB race") categories, which established four standard categories: White, Black, Asian/Pacific Islander, and American Indian/Alaska Native. The categories of UNESCO Race became the standard in government, science, and society.

Meanwhile, genetic science rapidly progressed. Since Darwin's time, geneticists had used family pedigree maps of bloodlines to track down health and disease-causing genes in humans. But now scientists were finding ways to isolate and analyze specific sequences of DNA within genes and learning to manipulate those sequences with new chemistry and informatic technologies. From the 1970s to the 1980s, modern genetics was eclipsed by "genomics"—the study of all the DNA sequences in an organism. With its high-resolution mapping of sequences handed down from generation to generation worldwide, genomic science would soon bring about its own paradigm of race.

Deploying novel techniques for mapping and cloning DNA, genome scientists learned a great deal about the basic mechanics of human DNA that apply to every person. They found that DNA—deoxyribonucleic acid—is the machinery in our cells that encodes all the proteins (the hormones, enzymes, antibodies, etc.) that we need to live. DNA is passed down to us from our ancestors via our parents' egg and sperm. All our cells have this same DNA code bunched up in the twenty-three chromosomes that lie in our cells' nuclei.*

IN 1986, DOUBLE HELIX discoverer James Watson and several other leading genome scientists working at the Salk Institute, US National Institutes of Health (NIH), and US Department of Energy (DOE) called for a global initiative to sequence a human genome, to produce a reference that anyone anywhere in the world could use to better understand DNA sequences. Many of these researchers were homing in on sequences associated with breast cancer and cancers caused by radiation, as well as other debilitating illnesses.

In 1989, Howard Hughes Medical Institute fellow Francis Collins used an innovative mapping technique he had developed to find the gene responsible for cystic fibrosis. Within months, his team and others around the world were able to pinpoint disease genes that had stumped geneticists for over a century. With this proof of concept, the federal

---

* There is also a tiny bit of DNA in the cells' mitochondria. Scientists refer to this as "mtDNA" or "mitochondrial DNA." In humans, mtDNA codes for thirteen proteins that supply cells with energy.

government swiftly moved to fund the proposed genome project, allocating three billion dollars to James Watson at the NIH and Director for Health and Environmental Research David J. Galas at the DOE.

Over the next couple years, seventeen nations joined the NIH and DOE to launch the first Human Genome Project. Watson and Galas soon passed leadership to Francis Collins and Ari Patrinos, leader of the DOE's Biological and Environment Research division. In these first years of the Human Genome Project, none of the project leaders discussed global diversity or race. They merely sourced DNA from the most convenient repositories on hand—those in northwestern Europe and the United States. At the same time, the Surgeon General and officials across America's chief public health departments such as the Department of Health and Human Services (HHS), Centers for Disease Control and Prevention (CDC), and Food and Drug Administration (FDA) were working hard to figure out how to implement OMB race in their operations. The Surgeon General and HHS had published reports about the long-overdue need for racial minorities' inclusion in health research and greater research into racial health disparities.

When the NIH mandated that all publicly funded researchers tabulate the race of their study participants in 1992, to ensure that US health science was fulfilling these briefs, the Human Genome Project was drawn into the existing discussions of race. The project and the wider field of genomics was now required to report the participation of study recruits according to the OMB taxonomy of race—White, Black, American Indian and Alaska Native, and Asian and Pacific Islander. Genome scientists had to decide just how they were going to sample DNA and affix racial data to it.

As the Human Genome Project entered its final phase in the mid-1990s, the Health Department extended OMB race to more US federal agencies that handled research abroad. Though global genome projects relied on collaboration by scientists and governments from all over the world, it was the NIH that initiated these projects, and the US government and leaders in American public health who often administered them. Therefore, every new project and many of their research offshoots came under the auspices of the US government's politics of race.

In 1997, the FDA also extended the use of OMB categories to drug research across the globe by requiring all new drug applications to tabulate safety and efficacy by OMB race. This meant that drug makers interested in marketing drugs on an international scale had to report dosage recommendations by the racial scheme that the OMB had concocted for social purposes.

Seeing that the project's own collection had no OMB data, that same year the NIH created a repository of samples that it gathered and stored using OMB race. This racially stratified "Polymorphism Discovery Resource" would become the basis for nucleotide mapping projects and research throughout government, academic, and industry science for years to come.

In 1998, the Human Genome Project began to study how race and ethnicity influenced uses and interpretations of genetic science, genetic services, and genetic policies. The project also funded a research grant to calculate how genomics was affecting group identity and societal beliefs about race. When later that year sequencing innovator Craig Venter left the NIH to spin off a startup to speed up the mapping process, his team deliberately sampled DNA from members of different OMB races to achieve global diversity in the project's newest collections.

In these final years of the twentieth century, the nascent field of genomics came under the microscope as the NIH worked to make the United States a leader in genomic science *and* diverse and equitable public health. Collins, Venter, and other leaders of the Human Genome Project began formulating a new understanding of race as socially constructed (formed in part by racial bias and racism), but in a way that can interact with our genetics. These leaders appeared in the international news media exclaiming that, without the social component, race was "a bogus idea" and that "ranking people" was something we needed to "get . . . out of our heads"; they called for using federal guidelines to bring racial minorities into genomics to better understand the diseases from which they suffered.

At a White House ceremony held in the East Room to commemorate the Genome Project's first draft of the human genome, President Bill Clinton remarked on the project's step forward for humankind, drawing attention to race: "In genetic terms, all human beings, regardless of race, are more than 99.9 percent the same." Collins and Venter joined Clinton, Britain's Prime Minister Tony Blair, and world leaders from Japan, China, Germany, and France in celebrating unity and denying inaccurate and harmful definitions of race. Collins delighted in sharing the news that "the only race we are talking about is the human race." Venter added, "The concept of race has no genetic or scientific basis." Yet within months, at a press conference, Collins issued a new statement on race that articulated the more nuanced genomic view implying that racial health disparities could be caused by legacies of gene–environment interactions accumulating disease disparities in different races over time. At the dawn of the new millennium, genome scientists celebrated that genomic science would finally address the most fundamental questions about the nature of race, the facts and fictions that described race as a social and genomic reality.

With the Human Genome Project's first mapping a new version of race dawned—"Genomic Race." Like Enlightenment Race, Genomic Race revolves around a fictitious continental-genetic scheme (White,

Black, Asian, Pacific Islander, Indigenous American), and, like Modern Race, it views all races as being human, descended from a single origin, and of a single species. But like UNESCO Race, Genomic Race considers genomic populations equally fit, no race superior to another. Still, unlike UNESCO Race, Genomic Race argues for research that combines social-environmental and genomic data to explain the amalgam of factors that make race real. It inadvertently positions its own science of gene–environment interactions—how DNA impacts and is impacted by social experiences—as what will reveal the varying physiologies and pathologies we see in today's races.

Scientists working in this paradigm believe in using genomics to illuminate the interaction of racial bias with genetic processes in the body—as many scientists say, how race gets "under the skin" and sickens us—making us more aware of the simultaneous social and biological nature of race. However, like the paradigms of yesteryear, Genomic Race fails to dismantle the genetically deterministic view of race. In using continental and quasi-continental schemes of inclusion and analysis like OMB race, it reinforces the belief that racial differences are due to our genetics.

AFTER THE HUMAN GENOME Project published the draft map in 2000, the NIH donated its OMB-classified Polymorphism Discovery Resource samples to a new project comprising the Human Genome Project's British sponsor, the Wellcome Trust, and thirteen pharmaceutical and biotech companies. These companies established The SNP Consortium, named for single nucleotide polymorphisms, often called SNPs (pronounced "snips"), which are the most common type of genetic variation among people. Their goal was to develop an applied map of the human genome that could be used to enhance our understanding of disease and help facilitate research. In little more than a year, The SNP Consortium located over a million genomic variants and showed that humans passed down segments of nucleotides in chunks: what researchers called "haplotypes." Genomic scientists rejoiced that they now had a clear path to understanding human diversity—to map these chunks of DNA in our cells. Haplotype mapping promised to shorten the process of finding genetic culprits of disease, requiring a fraction of the time and cost of other forms of genome mapping. It also promised to generate important information about race: to make it easier to compare DNA in people and groups all over the world, revealing the history of human evolution and migration. Haplotype mapping would finally tell us what global diversity meant in terms of disease disparities—which OMB races had which diseases, and why.

In 2002, the NIH and The SNP Consortium, along with the Wellcome Trust and governmental agencies in Canada, China, and Japan, launched the International HapMap Project (what I refer to as "HapMap"). Following OMB guidelines, HapMap attempted to collect DNA from people believed to be indigenous to various continents.

But not every community embraced that mission of DNA collection. Some Native American representatives from the Arhuaco, Chippewa, Lakota, Navajo, and Paiute nations protested genetic analysis of indigenous American DNA because they did not agree with prior genome project interpretations of DNA lineages. These groups rejected the idea that Native American peoples were part of a single genetic lineage or that a DNA test could prove a person's tribal membership. Especially given the government's use of blood quantum laws, which limited claims to citizenship or land based on a person's percentage of "native blood," genetic testing was and remains a fraught topic in many native communities.

Ultimately, HapMap decided to sample only DNA from Africa, Asia, and Europe, and to group those samples into continentally distinct collections. HapMap soon became the largest DNA repository in the world, one that scientists from nearly every country used in their research. This racialized database enabled Genomic Race to become the gold standard in health science worldwide.

HapMap's leadership—scientists like Aravinda Chakravarti, a codirector with Collins of the Polymorphism Discovery Resource; Eric Lander, head of Human Genome Project sequencing at Harvard and MIT; and David Altshuler, leader of The SNP Consortium— were extremely sensitive to the quandary of addressing race. They saw how eugenics had produced a health science that served only Whites, and how eugenics had structured modern medicine to exclude racial minorities from research and healthcare. As leaders in American public health, they determined to make genomics a diverse, equitable, and inclusive science; they understood that without a strong inclusionary program, the effects of drugs and treatments on communities with minority ancestries would remain understudied, as would their basic genetics.

Project leaders compelled external researchers using HapMap samples to report any analyses with labels that either noted the population origins from which the DNA had been sampled or an acronym of their preferred ethnic terms. In the case of DNA that the project grouped as "African," samples had to be referred to as "Bantu-speaking populations in Africa" or "YRI" for "Yoruba of Ibadan, Nigeria." DNA characterized as "Caucasian" was to be referred to as "populations in Europe" or "CEU" for "Utah residents with Northern and Western European ancestry from the CEPH collection." The DNA from individuals grouped as "Asian" was to be referred to as "populations in East

Asia" or "CHB/JPT" for "Han Chinese/Japanese." So, though project leaders attempted to communicate geographical and cultural specificity, by grouping collections by continent they prompted continental analysis and comparison according to OMB race. Genomic Race made race and genetics seem inextricably linked, while obscuring the social reality of race that it purportedly desired to expose.

HapMap's DNA collection and labeling perpetuated the long-standing misconception, inherited from Enlightenment Race, Modern Race, and UNESCO Race, that racial groups were genetically real. In terms of genetics, race is a fiction. However, race becomes socially real as we act on that fiction and our false beliefs about race.

Still, not all genomic research in the wake of the Human Genome Project perpetuated misconceptions about race. More in-depth haplotype mapping of groups living in Africa showed that all humans evolved from a single ancestor in sub-Saharan Africa, and that humans are indeed one unified species. It further showed that while humans migrated from the place where our first ancestor lived, in eastern Africa, to other parts of Africa, to the Middle East, and to Asia, Oceania, and the Americas, these voyagers made many return trips along the way. The research showed that humans have never been geographically separate enough to evolve discrete genetic, continent-spanning human types, much less races.

Tracing the lineages of specific haplotypes, researchers also showed that there are very few human groups that correspond to what scientists would call a distinct genetic population, or a "population isolate." Groups overlapped and intermixed, not remaining genetically distinct, mating only with people in their own culturally or geographically distinct group (what scientists call "endogamous"), as the term implies. Though a population isolate could potentially arise if a group has remained apart from the rest of the world—for example, a group living on a remote island with no inflow of outsiders, or one residing in a mountainous territory without migration—very few groups have ever remained so isolated.

Haplotype analyses have shown that even ethnic groups that scientists once assumed met the criteria for endogamy have less shared genetic ancestry than was previously believed. For example, a group once deemed a population isolate is the Parsi community. Parsis, who number in the 20,000s, comprise a group of Persians who migrated from ancient Iran to what is today India and Pakistan to practice their religion, Zoroastrianism. Another population isolate is the Sherpa community of Nepal and Tibet who, living in remote regions of the Himalayas, have adapted to the highest altitudes on the planet.

As technology has advanced, scientists have gotten a better look into the genomes of these groups, and some have retreated from identifying them as "isolates." Genomic analysis has shown that Parsis, for example, have been more cross-cultural than was previously known, and have been endogamous only periodically. Over half of their gene pool today can be attributed to ancestral DNA lineages common in other South Asian groups (as compared to Iranians who attribute less than 10 percent of their ancestral DNA to such lineages). Likewise, Sherpas display patterns of genetic ancestry similar to those of other Tibetan, Burmese, and Nepalese groups that are not considered isolates (blends of South and East Asian lineages).

In addition to debunking myths of isolation, haplotype analysis has shown that traits and diseases that were previously thought to only benefit or harm one group hailing from one specific continent are shared by others in faraway parts of the world. Rare traits, such as the ability to breathe at high altitude, exist in populations worldwide—

Europe, Asia, and the Americas—as do rare conditions: Black people aren't the only group who get sickle cell disease and Jewish people aren't the only group who get Tay-Sachs. The genomic prevalence of these rarities in so many populations shows how similarly humans have evolved in different parts of the world, how far we have traveled, and how much we have "mixed" with the humans we have encountered. For example, although we're used to seeing milk and cheese on menus across the globe, the ability to digest lactose is actually a rare trait. It's estimated that up to 75 percent of humans are lactose-intolerant. Some people may digest cow's milk easily and some people may not, but this trait doesn't correspond to any kind of "racial" difference.

Rare traits are sometimes shared by very distant and different peoples. In the case of high-altitude breathing, we see evolutionary similarities among Sherpas in the Himalayas and dwellers in the Andes. We can trace lactose tolerance in a number of ancient farming communities in Sweden, South India, and Sudan. Sickle cell disease is common among the ancestral populations of western and central Africa, India, the Arab Peninsula, the Mediterranean, and parts of South America, Central America, and the Caribbean. Tay-Sachs is prevalent among the Amish, Ashkenazi Jews, Cajun, and French Canadians, but has also been on the rise in Chinese populations for several decades.

All the high-resolution haplotype mapping has led genome scientists to formulate a new nomenclature of haplogroups, grouping similar haplotypes that have been shown to come from a common ancestor, and labeling them with letters and numbers ("U5," "M14," etc.). These codes refer to real sequences of DNA, not anything beyond that such as race or ethnicity, nationality or language, or even traits or diseases. Haplogroup M21a, associated with my mother's native northern Indonesian ancestry, for example, is but a small fragment of my larger genome. M21a does not encode specific genetic functions in me that would make me the same as everyone who has inherited DNA from Indonesia, and it most certainly does not make me the same as all others with Asian heritage (that is, all who share my race). Nor does M21a make me work differently than Kaiya, who is racialized as Black. Haplogroup EM2 is associated with Kaiya's African American ancestry. The EM2 haplogroup is one of many short sequences of DNA that is shared by some Black people's genomes but isn't present in the genome of all Black people. In other words, there is no common, universal "Black" DNA.

The neutral coding of haplogroups in alphanumeric sequences helps us avoid confusing haplogroups, which refer to genetic ancestry from very specific pinpoints on the globe, with continental race. No haplogroup is shared by all Indonesians or all African Americans, which challenges the notion that our genomes hold "Asian" or "Black" DNA. The diversity and admixture of haplogroups show that scientists should not group DNA samples or populations into discrete races as global genome projects have done, and that genomic research should not deploy the language of race as Genomic Race has done.

No matter how well-meant, using OMB race as a proxy for genetic variation is faulty because it inaccurately draws a genetic distinction between groups of people based on the continents their ancestors came from. These categories simply don't correspond to biological differences. From a genetic perspective, there is no logic to grouping people based on their identity as White, Black, American Indian or Alaskan Native, and Asian or Pacific Islander. There is a wide range of diversity within groups local to a continent, and there can be a large amount of similarity between groups across different continents. The inaccurate fixation on continental groupings of race then leads to a social and political reality that is incredibly harmful, as discussed in the following chapters. It allows the racist fiction of our earliest lies about human variation to continue to be made into social and political reality.

CHAPTER 3

Seeing and Thinking Race

As I witnessed genomic projects and studies vacillate between denouncing and deploying continental race, I began to dive deeper into the origins of this confusion. I wondered how racial labels kept finding their way back into genomic science even when the actual research had nothing to do with race. I found that in addition to wanting to diversify genomic datasets, project leaders were increasingly concerned with racial biases in science and the dynamics of race beyond the genetic realm, matters that leading social scientists were bringing to light with their own research. While all that illuminating genomics work was being done in the final decades of the twentieth century, social science research continued to unravel the complex knot of race in our society that so troubled Kaiya and me. Social scientists were revealing how race is created and enforced socially, how it is performed individually, and how it is absorbed and perpetuated in institutions. As the Human Genome Project and HapMap were in development, scholars in many fields demanded that race and racism receive attention, especially from health science researchers.

To understand the unwavering commitment to using genomics to determine what's real about race, we must look to the most influential social research models of race that took hold at the turn of the millennium. Social scientists studying colonization, enslavement, diaspora, and democracy called for all scientists to conduct research into racial differences and the racial structures of society. They denounced racial colorblindness—the ideology that the only way to eliminate racism is to ignore race and racial differences. Instead, they entreated experts to join them in illuminating how ideas of race structure our lives.

In the mid-1990s, sociologists Michael Omi and Howard Winant offered a highly influential framework for battling colorblindness when they coined the term "racial formations." This concept helped people see why racial systems of thought and practice exist, how they change, and why they rise and fall. Poring over the dense history of American political systems and the changing definitions of race from colonial times to the present, Omi and Winant found that race is a system of ideas that is constantly being transformed by human interactions. They showed that specific taxonomies and categories are, as they say, "created, inhabited, transformed, and destroyed." Racial formations are fabrications that, like shifting sands, change over time.

Seeing race in terms of formations helped experts in health science confront the endurance of racial systems of belief and the political nature of the work they were doing. As humans interacted based on Enlightenment Race, Modern Race, and UNESCO Race with the taxonomies advanced by Linnaeus or the OMB, race emerged as a social and political reality. And, as Omi and Winant reminded us, in countries with a long history of enslavement, like the United States, even seemingly benign choices (like deciding which care facilities to send patients to) and mundane interactions (like how to record a patient intake) reinforced political hierarchies. These minute interactions compound to create a vast system of segregated medicine and healthcare in which people of color are excluded from cutting-edge research and denied gold-standard therapies.

As Omi and Winant examined various formations of the past, they found that long after the end of American slavery, scientists and politicians continued to act in the interest of White supremacy. The racial formations of the Jim Crow era spurred more racist social interaction and more racist policies and laws. They determined where people lived, what kinds of resources they had access to, what their dwellings and facilities provided them—in other words, the real material reality of the world.

Moving on to the civil rights era, the Reagan era, and the post-Reagan era, Omi and Winant also found that, though the specifics changed, belief in the political salience of race held fast. Race has been defined as genetic, physiological, psychological, cultural, ethnic, socioeconomic, and imperial at different times in history. Yet changing from one definition to another has not diminished the power of race to condition our lives.

Likewise, though certain forms of government have changed, race's centrality to government has held fast. "WEIRD" (Western Education Industrialized Rich Democratic) nations such as Australia, Britain, Canada, and the United States, as well as the many countries that these nations colonized, were once ruled as racial dictatorships, or White supremacist states. Coercion was the governing principle, and enslavement, internment, incarceration, exploitation, and victimization were their mainstay methods. As these same governments have attempted to move toward "postcolonialism," or a form of government that rejects, if it does not redress, colonial oppression, they have continued to use old racial classification systems. Many have coined official racial taxonomies like OMB to monitor and fight racism, so race has intentionally remained a pillar of their social structure even as governments have moved away from overt White supremacy.

We learned from social analyses of racial formations that race does not have to be defined biologically or pejoratively to lead to racism. At the sunset of the twentieth century, most American experts on race defined it in terms of socioeconomics and culture, not genetics or biology. Similarly, Black, Indigenous, and other activists who were people of color engaged in antiracist political struggle in which they offered positive stereotypes about members of different races. Still, as British sociologist Paul Gilroy has pointed out, many antiracist scholars and activists have sustained the fiction of mutually exclusive races by claiming that there is a correct or culturally authentic, and therefore best, way to be a member of a particular race. Likewise, even some antiracist activists have promoted the notion of the superiority of Black and Brown bodies.

Just as the Human Genome Project leadership was reorienting the project to focus on the ethical, legal, and social implications of race in the late 1990s, Gilroy warned scientists that unwitting investments in race, what many call "racialism," perpetuated "false, destructive, or denigrating myths and ideas about race" even in the absence of any clear biological claim about racial difference or mention of hierarchy. Gilroy's rich histories of the African diaspora challenged fellow experts to create a deeper sociopolitical understanding of the ways in which people around the globe have been mixing throughout human history.

He suggested seeing humans as members of dynamic cultures in perpetual movement, always in diaspora, always changing. He held up figures like Bob Marley—a racially mixed transnational musician and freedom fighter—to show that there was no essential way to be, define, or classify by using race.

THE WIDESPREAD INFLUENCE OF Gilroy's notion of the potential risk of racism in antiracist politics pointed to a broader shift in expert thinking on race that was taking hold in the latter half of the 1990s. Experts now understood that there could be racialism without racism—people could believe in genetic differences in races without believing in the supremacy of one of those races. Sociologist Stuart Hall's concept of race as a "floating signifier" explained why. Hall told us that the mechanisms of racialism arise from race being a perpetually changing signifier—words that stand in for many different meanings and that mean many different things (both positive and negative) to anyone who is using them. Race is constantly being redefined by people in positions of authority and is also being reclaimed by those resisting that authority by using the same categories. When activists petition for a Black History month or schools introduce an Asian Pacific Heritage curriculum, seeking political recognition for certain categories forces those antiracist activists to use the same terminology to fight back. This has made fighting racism more complicated than simply telling people to stop noticing or denigrating the color of someone's skin. The floating signifier of race has remained strong in our minds whether or not we have thought about others in prejudiced ways.

Hall's work dovetailed with Indian postcolonial scholar Gayatri Spivak's theory of "strategic essentialism," the practice of temporarily playing into an overly simplistic characterization of race for political purposes. Experts like Hall and Spivak, who had affiliations with multiple cultural and national milieus and were fighting racism in widely differing political contexts, found that fighting racism takes a revolutionary act of raising a new consciousness among minoritized people as well as members of the dominant group. When Gilroy and Hall popularized the term "Black British" in the late 1990s, they did so to unify a diverse group of people under one shared identity and to teach a new way of thinking. Pairing the seemingly contradictory terms Black and British—colonized and colonizer, subjugated and subjugator—they reminded us that uttering the word "race" and speaking about racial injustice requires us to see the relationships between categories (the boxes or labels) and groups (the people the boxes refer to).

Far from eliminating the language of race, these scholars directed experts and activists to use racial designations as a political organizing tool, to repurpose the language of race to pose a new definition of race that temporarily presents minoritized groups as real, knowing full well that groupness is a fiction. Scholars like Gilroy, Hall, and Spivak believed that minimizing group differences while maximizing group similarities was the only hope to repurpose former categories of domination into empowering features of people's identities and offering points of organization for groups.

THE THEORIES OF RACE as a floating signifier and of strategic essentialism inspired many social researchers to distinguish not just between racialism—the belief that there are significant racial differences—and racism but also between two kinds of racism: prejudice and structural racism. Prejudice refers to the racist beliefs and perceptions held by individual people, people who see the world in terms of superiority and inferiority and who discriminate based on skin color and other stereotypical racial characteristics. Structural racism refers to the systemic nature of racial beliefs and perceptions, and the everyday onslaught of discrimination that follows from them.

Studying structural racism revealed some key dimensions of racism that explain why it is so tenacious despite our best efforts to fight it. Racism is institutionalized. It permeates our everyday social institutions—education, employment, healthcare, housing, and so on—and through these institutions, race is being enacted and made real. For example, Black, Latinx, and Indigenous youth who are more likely to live in poverty are also more likely to attend under-resourced schools and receive treatment from under-resourced medical facilities than all other youth in America. Likewise, they are more likely to be disciplined, confined, and referred to law enforcement, and less likely to be treated on an outpatient basis for mental illness, in grade school.

Racism is also intersectional—that is, compounded by other belief systems that fuel discrimination. Classism, sexism, heterosexism (what people often call "homophobia"), gender binarism, and other toxic "isms" link up with racism to elevate some in society and push others down. For example, Black women in the United States have the highest maternal mortality rates of any population, which is due to a combination of sexist reproductive inequality and racist medical injustice.

Racism is, moreover, "imperceptible." A person might feel the effects of discrimination mentally and physiologically, like the stress of trying to learn and achieve in a resource-poor school, or the terror of parenting a child who, because of the color of his skin, may become the target of police violence. But people often suffer the stress without being aware of it, let alone attributing it to racism. Likewise, other impacts of discrimination hit minoritized people in unseen biological ways, such as the slow deterioration of bodies that have been deprived of quality food and healthcare. Most dangerous are the invisible and acute exposures that threaten people's lives: the pathogens, viruses, and hazardous substances encountered on polluted job sites, or the mismanagement of the water supply in disadvantaged municipalities. For example, Black and Indigenous youth in cities around the world have higher asthma rates than others due to developers constructing public schools and housing near polluted highways and industrial zones.

Racism is intergenerational too. It endures across the generations, increasing gaps in all aspects of life even as societies try to restructure in more equitable ways. In many countries, like my home countries of Indonesia and the United States, schools were segregated by law until the 1950s, yet after that education continued to disadvantage people of color, so that educational disparities persisted even after racial segregation. Even at the zenith of school integration in the late 1980s, approximately half of White Americans obtained a college degree, while only about a quarter of Black Americans did. And in Dutch-colonized Indonesia, Whites were the only people permitted to attend college until Indonesians gained independence in 1945. But even in subsequent years of integrated education, little more than 10 percent of all local Indonesians have obtained a college degree.

Healthcare facilities such as hospitals and maternity wards, which were reserved for Whites deep into the twentieth century in most places in the world, were eventually integrated by law. Yet even integrated facilities continue to generate stark disparities in healthcare delivery for Whites and people of color. In nearly all countries that collect data on race, vital statistics indicate that minoritized groups still have poorer natal outcomes, with drastically higher infant and maternal mortality rates and lower life expectancies than Whites.

Until the late 1970s, many governments limited military benefit bills, farming and housing grants, business subsidies, and educational stipends to Whites, affording poor and working Whites class mobility. Yet even as policies were extended to people of color in the late twentieth century, past grants and subsidies compounded wealth for Whites. In the United Kingdom today, for example, the average White household has approximately double the wealth of the average Black household and generally holds a larger share of assets.

Labor markets in corporate America, higher education, and other lucrative economic domains remained shut to most people of color as well, spawning racial wage gaps and ensuring that professions that generate wealth and power would continue to be dominated by Whites into the twenty-first century. Even in industries where unions and professional associations have been successful in desegregating occupations, a Black, Latinx, or Indigenous worker still makes less than 75 cents to a White person's dollar.

Into the final decades of the twentieth century, consumer markets increasingly targeted people of color with known toxins, such as cigarettes, sugary drinks, and junk food. The tobacco industry saw a vulnerability from which it could profit and predatorily advertised to Black, Asian, Latinx, and Indigenous people around the world through cultural events and youth programs, and even subsidized school programs, reserving its deadliest products for minoritized people. As a result, even today, as smoking-cessation campaigns make strides in communities around the world, racial minorities continue to experience far higher smoking-related addiction and death rates than Whites.

Neighborhoods, and the very living spaces that we call home, reflect all these hierarchies in consumption, opportunity, attainment, and intergenerational wealth, with racialized neighborhoods in the same cities showing life expectancy gaps of up to sixteen years between Whites and people of color, and White households averaging ten times the wealth of non-White households. Every building block of society, and of our lives, is a place of everyday racism, even when we don't see or hear overt prejudice.

THE GROWING BODY OF research on the differences between prejudice and structural racism left many researchers wondering whether social institutions that are governed by antiracist policy and are implementing antiracist measures, as science did, could perpetuate racism. Were latent prejudices at work? At the close of the century, Harvard psychologist Mahzarin Banaji decided to find answers by testing herself, and developed the now well-known implicit bias test.

Banaji and her colleague Tony Greenwald set up a computer experiment in which she was supposed to push one button whenever she saw a dark-skinned face or a negative word (e.g., *devil* or *war*) on the screen, and another button when she saw a light-skinned face or a positive word (e.g., *love, good*). This was an easy form of sorting, accomplished swiftly.

Then they switched the buttons so that Banaji had to press the first button when she saw a dark-skinned face and positive words, and the second button when she saw light-skinned faces and negative words. She was paralyzed by the challenge and could not master the test. Her brain associated the white faces with positive words more quickly and easily than it associated the dark-skinned faces with positive words. In essence, racial bias had trained her brain to have negative associations with darker-skinned people. Banaji and Greenwald determined that implicit biases could exist where we least expect them—even in the mind of an antiracist scientist working in an antiracist research lab.

Banaji, Greenwald, and their colleague Brian Nosek deployed the test widely and confirmed their suspicion. Comparing implicit bias test results to a participant's explicit biases—biases they voiced out loud—the team found that there were far more implicit biases than explicit ones. These implicit biases often contradicted what people explicitly said about race and influenced their social interactions, including whether they undertook racist acts. In other words, many people, like Banaji, who valued racial equality in their words also harbored implicit racial biases. Regardless of people's purported values, their implicit biases could better predict how they were going to treat others than could their stated preferences or opinions. Doctors who had high levels of implicit bias and low levels of explicit bias, for example, were less likely to prescribe the right treatment to their patients.

In 1998, Banaji, Greenwald, and Nosek established Project Implicit, an online research site that gathers data on the prevalence of racial bias in the American populace. Every seven or eight years, the project issues overarching reviews of data showing that implicit biases against Blacks and for Whites pervade America, and predicts that based on these biases, discriminatory behavior will continue to plague our society. The reviews, which have coincidentally corresponded with the passage of new global genome projects, have revealed that over 70 percent of Americans hold implicit biases. The same statistic applies to physicians, showing the importance of monitoring racial bias in all social institutions, especially health science and healthcare.

The growing body of implicit bias research has exposed several facts that impact how scientists view race. The first is that implicit bias is not consciously manifested or explicitly taught. Rather, it comes from living in a racist culture. Children as young as six years old exhibit implicit preferences for Whites regardless of their racial background and positive messages that they may have heard about themselves from their family and community, or their "ingroup." In fact, children of color who according to other measures exhibit a preference for their ingroup still maintain negative cultural stereotypes about their own group and accept stereotypes that celebrate Whites. Even children who show low levels of explicit bias and high comprehension of antiracist norms exhibit implicit bias. This tells us that despite the antiracist messages that children may encounter at home, they are being bombarded with racist messages from the media and the social institutions that structure their lives.

Second, stereotypes based on emotions, like fear, lodge in our memories more easily and are harder to unlearn. Research has shown that children learn racial stereotypes in their earliest years of life when they are most sensitive to fear-based imprinting. They end up developing a fear response to people with darker skin and this remains with them even when they enter explicitly antiracist environments.

Third, implicit biases lead people to commit racist acts no matter how little explicit bias they exhibit. Research into microaggressions, like subtle racial insults and assaults, revealed that these are most often subconscious, driven by implicit rather than explicit bias. What's worse, health practitioners and health researchers routinely commit microaggressions in clinical encounters without being aware of it. A nurse who may believe himself to be accepting, or antiracist, may be less responsive to reports of pain in Black children than in White children, due to implicit bias. Experts studying disease disparities, or differences in disease rates and progressions between different racial groups, now attribute inequities that they see to implicit bias, calling it a leading cause of health disparities.

STUDIES INTO THE NEUROSCIENCE of racial bias, stereotyping, and ingroup and outgroup classification that followed from Project Implicit in the early 2000s, as HapMap was getting underway, confirmed these findings, revealing another component of how we make race real to ourselves in our minds. Brain scans and other forms of body imaging showed how biases, stereotypes, and classifications become unwittingly embedded in brain circuitry. These studies showed that ideas of race are formed when we're young and impressionable, and they root strongly in us because they are tied to fear. Studies also showed that we often use categories of race to relate to one another even when we hold antiracist views and know that those categories aren't scientifically valid.

One thread of the research focused on the fear-governing part of the brain, the amygdala. When a person senses a threat, the amygdala activates the brain and body into "fight or flight" mode via the hypothalamus-pituitary-adrenals (HPA) axis. Research revealed that even the mere act of seeing people of other races promotes greater activity in various regions of the brain. Studies noted especially high elevated blood oxygen levels for White study participants viewing images of Black people. And these scans found increased activity in the amygdala for all those viewing images of people of color no matter whether the viewer was White or a person of color.

Another thread of research about neuroscience and race focused on the timing of neural activity across regions of the brain that are responsible for permitting different kinds of thoughts to arise. Studies found that images of people of color kick the amygdala and HPA axis into fight-or-flight mode before the rational parts of our brains, like the prefrontal cortex, can supply antiracist messaging. Similarly, studies showing images of people suffering demonstrated that the amygdala and HPA axis are triggered before other brain regions that are responsible for empathy (such as the anterior cingulate cortex and anterior insula) are able to process that a person is in pain. This timing sequence means that our brains cannot critically make sense of what we are seeing until *after* we have felt what we are seeing. Biased thoughts or fear will always be faster than antiracist reasoning and processing.

This neuroimaging research coincided with other bodies of research into stereotyping and categorization showing that colorblindness, being blind to race, isn't possible in a society awash in racial stereotypes. A subset of this research looked at fear-based imprinting in babies and toddlers, when they are forming their initial impressions of other people. Studies found that young children develop the neural processes that support categorization by race alongside their general fear-based conditioning of same versus other. This makes racial categorization and racial stereotyping a knee-jerk response, self-reinforcing and tenacious in young minds.

Research similarly showed that we have a better memory for faces of people that are the same race as us. Neuroimaging studies of facial recognition revealed that the fusiform gyrus, the part of the brain that has evolved to categorize what we see in order to identify threats, works differently depending on which race we believe we are perceiving. It also works more vigorously when we are viewing ingroup members, suggesting that we not only recognize ingroup faces more accurately but also with more intensity. When it comes to race, this increased recognition promotes greater activity in participants' memory networks, giving them what researchers call a "memory advantage for same-race faces." Researchers have concluded that participants see ingroup members as individuals and outgroup members as a homogenous "other." Moreover, outgroup homogeneity is self-reinforcing, and leads to increased stereotyping, decreased empathy, and an increased likelihood of discrimination, harm, and violence toward outgroup members.

At a turning point for genomic science, when health scientists were deciding whether to embrace OMB race or reject it, this mass of studies showed them that prejudice runs far too deep to ignore, that race is a reality and it is ubiquitous. All our social institutions, from education and employment to medicine and healthcare, are riddled with implicit biases. Even when we aren't aware that we hold biases, we often do. We learn race at such a young age that we end up automatically seeing and thinking it, reinforcing it in our minds and collectively through our social behavior. Race is a fiction that is made structurally real in our systems and institutions, and implicitly real in our minds, as we perceive and interact in all these arenas. There is no option to be colorblind in a society that collectively believes in race, because structural racism and implicit bias continually reinforce the social reality of race.

As I explain in the next chapter, leading genomic scientists hurried to implement OMB race in The SNP Consortium and the International HapMap Project so that they could reject colorblindness in science and recruit people of color into genomic research. However, their efforts arguably ended up perpetuating racial stratification in science. From its public release at the end of 2003 to summer 2005, HapMap's racialized dataset was downloaded over 500,000 times by researchers in over one hundred countries. Its meteoric rise motivated

Francis Collins and other public health leaders to embark on a new project to deliver the next generation of genomic sequencing: a whole-genome resource comprising a thousand unique genomes that they would call the "1000 Genomes Project."

With the 1000 Genomes Project, there was a fresh opportunity for leaders in genomics to question their use of OMB race and to reject the equation of genetic ancestry with continental race. Mapping an individual's genome would give scientists all the information about that person's unique genetics, so there would be no need to use racial categories in this analysis.

Yet, in the 1000 Genomes Project, leaders again followed NIH protocol in structuring their DNA database by continental race. They chose social policy over scientific validity, and once again reinforced false ideas about race.

CHAPTER 4

The Politics of Science

THE BIG IDEAS FROM SOCIAL science about structural racism and implicit bias made a huge impact on me as an emerging scholar of race with a deep passion for equity in science. How were those ideas being used in genetics and medicine? Social scientists were seeking to reveal the truth about race and its impact on our lives, while genomic scientists were trying to understand the relationship between our genes and our social environments to unravel the assumption that race and DNA were synonymous and rewrite harmful narratives about race. Were we finally gaining a bold understanding of what's real about race?

I came to see that nearly all the leaders in these fields were passionate about dispelling any belief that genetic populations and races were the same thing. And yet these elite scientists were equally passionate about preventing genomics from becoming just another color-blind science. Inclusion, representation, and involvement of all races was now a priority. Genomic scientists were using OMB categories in their research as well as advocating for genomic studies that could better explain the relationship between race and genetics.

As the 1000 Genomes Project was unfolding in the late aughts, I conducted research interviews with leaders of global human genome projects, spoke with genome scientists in the private sector and in companies that were changing the field with major technological and market breakthroughs. Nearly all of them rejected the notion of genetic races yet nearly all supported the use of racial categories like Asian, Black, and White in certain parts of the research process to communicate with and refer to research participants, to discuss and classify DNA samples, and to sort and disseminate DNA collections. Rejecting racial analysis in some parts of research and using OMB race categories in other parts created a contradiction. Should scientists include race in the study of the human genome? Or should they ignore it entirely?

One person I spoke with was Francis Collins, who was then director of the Human Genome Project, the Polymorphism Discovery Resource, the International HapMap Project, and the NIH National Human Genome Research Institute, as well as a major sponsor of The SNP Consortium and the 1000 Genomes Project. Collins explained to me that the field's leadership had to "get race right" by making responsible uses of racial classification and by remaining explicit about any misuses of racial classification. He was concerned that if genome scientists did not use OMB categories to recruit minorities into research to solve the puzzle of genetics and race, medical researchers and healthcare providers who had little understanding of genomes would continue to use race as a substitute for genetics, and people in the wider society would continue assuming that races were simply genetic populations.

Craig Venter, who was then working with Ari Patrinos on a new startup, agreed. When Venter's former firm, Celera, entered the race to complete a full sequence of a human genome, Venter took a population-based approach, seeking to achieve representation of the world's diversity by grouping populations by continental geography. While he didn't agree with the use of the term "race," he told me that representation of diverse "ethnogeographic" groups was "important *symbolically*" to the Human Genome Project. He conveyed the importance of battling colorblindness at all costs, explaining that the need for minority inclusion outweighed the risks of the public believing that genetic diversity equaled racial diversity. Venter argued that it was critical that scientists "use our power, our positions if we have any, to try and influence the world around us." He also told me that he was "ashamed of" and "extremely bothered by" humanity's history of inequality.

Venter also expressed the prevailing view that genomic science would be a better interpreter of the reality of race than other fields. To Venter, other disciplines, like zoology, had come up short. He hoped that more leaders in genomics would join him in making genomic science a guiding light for the public by revealing the truth about race. He believed that genomics would eventually unlock the best way for scientists to use racial classifications respectfully in research and reporting. He saw genomics—the first science able to analyze the interaction between genes and social environments, combining knowledge of our genetic reality with knowledge of our social reality—as a natural place for best practices to emerge.

To fight for a new kind of science, genome mappers believed that projects like the International HapMap Project and the 1000 Genomes Project needed to set new priorities. With a keen understanding of the dual perils of implicit bias and colorblindness in science and society, social justice was of supreme concern. The work of a genomic researcher now required thinking about minority representation, understanding the identities and identity politics that people of color in America and throughout the world experienced, and considering the litany of sociopolitical issues that could arise in the process of inclusion.

HapMap leader Eric Lander told me that he saw political matters, like classifying and labeling in socially responsible ways, as inextricable from the scientific process. He recounted how HapMap strategically represented humanity's diversity to ensure inclusion. To Lander, being inclusive meant deliberately and carefully seeking out groups in Africa, Asia, Europe, and the Americas.

The 1000 Genomes Project director David Altshuler echoed Lander in saying that understanding politics was, in fact, part of the genome scientist's job. He told me that HapMap chose particular groups to stand in for each continental grouping—for example, Ibadan Yoruba, North American Europeans, Tokyo Japanese, and Beijing Chinese—to ensure the utmost respect for and sensitivity toward racial minorities. As he put it, these choices were "purely practical" in the effort to include underserved racial groups made for "political, more than scientific" reasons.

In 2008, Luigi Luca Cavalli-Sforza, author of *Genes, Peoples, and Languages*, wrote a counterargument to using race in genomics, stating that "populations that are geographically close have an overwhelming genetic similarity, well beyond that suggested by continental or pseudocontinental partitions." Cavalli-Sforza, who had spearheaded the Human Genome Diversity Project in the early 1990s with a DNA collection from cultures around the world, was responding to two developing trends. One was genomic science's turn toward creating clinical applications—what scholars were calling the "bench to bedside" translation of genomic science into genomic medicine and healthcare. The other was the reinscription of OMB by scientists battling colorblindness, which I have been calling Genomic Race.

Cavalli-Sforza told me that he wanted to warn epidemiologists and others who were implementing genomics in medical labs and clinics against seeing and thinking race. He was troubled that scientists working with genomic data were labeling DNA by OMB race, publishing results by race, and joining journalists in using race as a shorthand when reporting findings to the public. His attempt to discourage the use of OMB categories was unsuccessful. At the close of the 2000s, the notion of Genomic Race was fully established across the field of genomics.

SEEING RACE AND USING OMB categories were important to genomic scientists in terms of research recruitment and also personnel recruitment. In fact, leaders of global projects like HapMap and the 1000 Genomes Project saw the two forms of recruitment as interdependent. In conversation with me, in their internal deliberations, and in their communiqués to the public, they emphasized the importance of having scientists of color at the forefront of genomic research. They wanted the most "relatable" scientists to engage community leaders to show that those lending their DNA to research were being adequately involved in research decision making. Positioning scientists of color on the front lines demonstrated that their genome projects were identifying and training scientists with kinship to the populations under study. Project leaders wanted as many community-based scientists to do the actual recruitment and sampling as possible. One strategy involved hiring foreign-born scientists of color to oversee the training of local scientists; another was to deploy US- or UK-based minority scientists to sample populations who shared their racial identity.

This push for a definitive genomics of race—what researchers believed would be the world's first genuine understanding of the reality of race—enabled more genome scientists to be vocal about racial inequality. However, even those who shared with me stories of their intensive efforts to advance a complex and critical perspective on race ultimately reinforced OMB classification and Genomic Race with their work. HapMap's Africa branch was led by Nigerian scientist Charles Rotimi, the founder of the National Human Genome Research Center—the world's first African American genomic research institute—at one of America's premier historically black colleges and universities, Howard University. Rotimi leveraged his position to fight for Black inclusion in genomic research and analysis of diseases that disproportionately affected Black people in Africa and the Americas. After establishing HapMap's Nigerian base in 2003, he attempted the first race-based genome project in the world: the African American Diversity Project. Though Rotimi's growing commitments at HapMap and the NIH forestalled getting his own project off the ground, a few years later, he launched the NIH's first trans-institute center on the genomics of racial health disparities and founded the Human Heredity and Health in Africa Project (H3Africa), concentrating on sub-Saharan African genomics. Though Rotimi's intention was to dispel harmful genetic notions of race, his efforts ensured that Genomic Race, which holds a continental-genetic notion of race at its core, would be the authoritative paradigm in science and public health.

Rotimi recounted to me his racial awakening in the United States, first as husband of a descendant of formerly enslaved people and then as a researcher at Howard University. He constantly had to shift between various kinds of racial awareness: as social elite in his home country, as Black person in the United States, as father to African American children, and as person of color in the global context. He said he could not conduct colorblind science because his life was race-conscious. Echoing Collins, Venter, and Lander, Rotimi spoke of how genomics would be the best place to gain a new understanding of race. He believed that, through their research, genome scientists would find the right way of handling classification systems with the utmost care, while modeling the best way to be vocal as scientists to ensure others got it right too.

In a similar vein, HapMap's China branch was led by Chinese scientist Piu Yan Kwok. When we met, Kwok was just forming the Human Variome Project—an OMB-structured genomic database powered by Google that would crowdsource genomic research. Kwok did the essential work of engaging communities and setting up research sites in their home countries. He shared how critical it was for his projects to take a race-focused approach, using OMB race as a guide in recruiting and considering race politics at the earliest moments of research design and at every subsequent step along the way.

Kwok relayed to me stories of learning what it meant to be Asian in a non-Asian country. In the United States he had to start seeing skin color, and to prioritize doing so, because race was so politically charged in his day-to-day life there. In China, he noticed the traits he had been taught to value as a kid, like facial contours and the length of earlobes, but in the United States seeing race required a different kind of optics. He felt it was a disservice to his patients and research subjects to remain colorblind.

I watched as across the field minoritized scientists spoke up publicly about their struggles and healing through learning about genomics. In their many visits to community centers, appearances on television, and high-profile publicized speaking events, scientists of color shared how their work in genomics illuminated the senselessness of stereotypes. CEO and founder of the first direct-to-consumer African genomics biotech firm, African Ancestry Inc., Rick Kittles, exclaimed to me, and to his audiences at community-based meetings, that Black people weren't all genetically identical. As he told me, "All Blacks do not like chicken and watermelon! All Blacks do not have the same Duffy allele [blood group classification]!"

Similar passion arose in Kittles's colleague Esteban Burchard, a leader in Latinx pulmonary disease research at UCSF. Burchard described how important it was for members of the Latinx community to enroll in studies so that they wouldn't get left behind in the genomic revolution. For him, hunting for asthma genes in Latinx people was like "love at first sight" because it afforded him the opportunity to work for the community he loved and find the culprits for the diseases that plagued his people. Burchard highlighted how genomic research bestowed that "aha moment" that illuminated how much race and racism can impact health and revealed the dangers of colorblind science.

THE MANY SCIENTISTS THAT I spoke with were using their position to reveal the nuanced truth about race to the public. Countless times, they publicized the view that though researchers must use OMB's White, Black, Asian, Pacific Islander, American Indian/Alaska Native classifications to recruit research subjects for political reasons of inclusion, OMB is still a poor proxy for genetics. And yet, in their research, it appeared that genetic populations and OMB races were one and the same. As I struggled to understand how people so committed to racial justice could perpetuate the misconception that races are genetic populations, I uncovered another thread of racial reinforcement: publishing research results by race. In structuring research projects, studies, and DNA collections by OMB race, scientists were perpetuating a system of analyzing and reporting by race as if races each had a mutually exclusive, distinct genetic makeup, which they obviously do not.

In the 2000s, preeminent publications such as *Science*, *New England Journal of Medicine*, and *Nature Genetics* developed guidelines that systematically supported racial or quasi-racial classification and analysis using OMB, or continental labels that correspond to OMB. In practice, analyses of DNA samples that might or might not already have been racialized often became so in publication. Reporting by OMB classification made it appear that OMB groups have their own genetic ancestry and their own genetic diseases.

The project scientists who I began working with in the late aughts, and others I came to work closely with subsequently, had published op-eds, convened public meetings to produce statements on race, and written books on the topic. Yet, in debating whether to use OMB classifications in all genomic research recruitment and reporting or only in research recruitment (in other words, to recruit racial minorities and then remove OMB labels from DNA samples), the scientific community and scientific publishing community came to an agreement that some form of racial analysis and reporting by OMB classification was necessary.*

Through the latter half of the 2000s, scientific journals asked researchers to report the rationale behind their study labels to counter any notion that race was genetic. Yet in advocating descriptors that their readership could recognize and understand, many journals ended up mandating racial and quasi-racial labeling. They featured their own

---

* Genome scientists advanced two less popular positions in the aughts: that OMB races were a good proxy for continental-genetic populations and that genomic research should never deploy racial categories. Though these positions garnered media attention, they did not inform policy.

brands of continental or color-coded language, like "White" versus "Black," or "European American" versus "Asian." As one former editor put it, "There is a high and useful degree of correlation between ethnicity/race and genetic structure," so it would be "unwise to abandon the practice of recording race." Evidently these editors understood that there was a problem with invoking race in genetic terms, but they were still comfortable using racial or quasi-racial categories in science reporting. And though many scientists I spoke with took issue with the claim that OMB race was a useful stand-in for "genetic structure," few pushed back against journal policies.

Racial classification within scientific journals continued to rise in the wake of the global genome projects and has been on the rise ever since. In a study I conducted with Aaron Panofsky, director of the Institute for Society and Genetics, we found that over a period of almost two decades at the turn of the twenty-first century, genetic reports in the journal *Nature Genetics* had gone from very little population labeling to nearly ubiquitous labeling, with the greatest growth in quasi-racial continental labeling that was nearly indistinguishable from OMB race. Labels such as Asian, African, and European leapt from the page at every turn.

We also found that scientists used all kinds of descriptors, sometimes differently within a single study. Titles and abstracts might have one label, often quasi-racial ("Africa" or "East Asia and Europe"), and the introduction and conclusion a similar one to convey the gist of the study's findings ("East Asians found to have . . . "). But looking at other sections, such as Methods or Supplemental Methods, we often saw completely different labels, often nonracial ("DNA from the people of Ibadan, Nigeria"). One article we dissected, for example, had sixteen labels utilized differently in thirty-three instances in eight sections of the paper, whose title included an OMB label.

It was no surprise that press offices, journalists, and science writers covered such studies in stark racial terms ("Whites possess . . ."). Over and over again, reports on DNA collected from relatively isolated groups such as the Masai were simplified by the media so the findings were applied to anyone Black, that Whites were more genetically susceptible to aggressive forms of breast cancer while Asians were more genetically susceptible to lung cancer or Blacks to aggressive forms of prostate cancer. Others assigned different kidney diseases, metabolic disorders, and mental illnesses to different racial groups. Though the only science-backed racial comparisons came from studies on the social determinants of health, not genetics, the output of major media implied that genomic analysis proved races had entirely different genes and diseases.

When I interviewed genome scientists on what they thought about the chaos in categorization, I found that they not only embraced the disarray but thrived on it. The elite, who wield a great deal of power and routinely engage in public outreach, wanted as much leeway as possible to articulate their own labels. They wanted to be able to use racial and quasi-racial labels in subject recruitment, and to use other kinds of labels, like ethnic or linguistic, when referring to DNA sequences. They also wanted to use racial or quasi-racial, or even nationalistic labels in reporting if their research subjects wanted them to do so. This freedom enabled them to align their reporting with their subjects' self-determined political labels, for example, using the participants' term "African American" instead of "East" or "West African." They needed labeling to be ambiguous and flexible from the earliest stages of recruitment to the latest stages of publication so they could maintain their authority over the research process. As a result, they allowed for slippages in labeling even when those slippages seemed contradictory.

Talking with these scientists recently, I have come to sympathize with their struggles as researchers walking a tightrope plaited with strands of population categorization, political representation, and interpersonal respect. But I have also concluded that label slippage confuses the public about the meaning of race and can introduce misinformation that fuels existing racism. There are many horrifying examples of the harm caused by misinterpreting genomic science, such as when, in 2022, after citing genomic research in a manifesto posted to Google and Discord, nineteen-year-old Payton Gendron livestreamed himself killing ten and wounding three Black shoppers at a Tops Friendly supermarket in Buffalo, New York. He had misinterpreted study findings to mean that races had different intellectual aptitudes. But there are also many more subtle examples of misinformation that endangers people of color, such as when a doctor misreads a genomic study report that suggests a racial finding where there isn't one and then mistreats a patient accordingly. Research into physicians' knowledge about genetics and race, as well as their prescription practices by race, shows that physicians' misunderstandings about genetics and race hurt their ability to diagnose and treat patients of color, and poor medical outcomes widen racial health gaps.

So, although today's leading genome scientists have attempted to divert our attention and resources away from old-school notions of race, and many of them have tried to get us thinking in more complicated terms, decades out from HapMap and the 1000 Genomes Project we are still steeped in a genetics of race. We still see research and reporting awash in race in ways that harm the very groups we intend to help.

There have been other grave but perhaps less obvious barriers to scientists' inclusionary work. Yes, genomic researchers have been vocal about "Eurocentrism" (biases favoring the inclusion of Whites and their needs and perspectives), criticizing past scientists for studying Whites only and advising other scientists on how to "really [do] enough to engage minority populations," as some minoritized genome mappers have entreated. But those who study genomics focus on access to cutting-edge science, rather than on dismantling racism across medicine and healthcare.

All too frequently, inclusion in a research project, such as giving people of color the chance to donate their own DNA to a study, is considered a sufficient achievement. But if we compare research inclusion to civil rights organizing to desegregate medicine and healthcare, or to the creation of alternative minority-owned healthcare systems, we realize just how insufficient research inclusion is. It does not increase access to basic healthcare, not to mention quality healthcare, and it does nothing to prevent the daily onslaught of racism that threatens people of color and leads to poorer health outcomes.

There is harm in equating race-based research inclusion with racial equity. As scientists of color have appealed to laypeople of color to get involved with DNA research, they have inadvertently created racially siloed databases on a par with the siloed collections of the major international genome projects. This reservoir of data has only enabled the systemic practice of comparing the DNA of races as if they were genetically distinct populations—Africans versus Europeans versus Asians and so on.

So, when African Ancestry's Rick Kittles says, "When I go into West Africa, people see themselves in what I do and I make sure of that," or when HapMap's Rotimi says you need to "understand this community" and you need "somebody that they can relate to, to participate in a study like this," we must question the endpoint of research inclusion.

As Alondra Nelson, former director of the White House Office of Science and Technology Policy, has warned, "authentic expertise" can be a double-edged sword if it is used to bring the racially oppressed into an even more genetically deterministic system that does nothing to challenge the social structures that cause oppression in the first place.

Despite complaining about the misuse of racial categories in genetic science, and promising not to use race as a proxy for genetic variation, genomic scientists have largely preserved racial classifications. Tying research findings to OMB or quasi-OMB categories belies the scientists' goal of ensuring a diversity of samples while maintaining the distinction between race and genetic ancestry. Allying themselves with racial justice advocacy organizations like the NAACP, scientists have declared research-subject self-identified race and ethnicity (what many call "SIRE") to be the modus operandi of genomics. They argue that minority groups must determine their own sense of group identity, and that choice must be elevated in the research process from recruitment to reporting. As Mark Shriver, forensic expert and inventor of DNA face-profiling, says, "We don't want to insult the people who are being sampled . . . by using completely academic terms . . . or terms that they find offensive!" However, as we have seen, reporting with racial terms only leads to racial conclusions and inaccurate descriptions that fuel more misunderstanding in science and the public.

In reviewing studies that have followed from race-based DNA sampling campaigns, I have found that very few have collected information on social, cultural, or socioeconomic factors, and there is little to no research out there on racism. As Elad Ziv, the UCSF oncologist who has worked closely with Latinx specialist Esteban Burchard to use OMB to enlist California Bay Area residents of color to genomic studies in that region, has said, using SIRE "tells you a lot about social aspects or cultural aspects of that person or sometimes it correlates with socioeconomic things." Yet research on samples referred to as "Black" or "Latino" has been used in the opposite way. Researchers have mostly ignored social, cultural, and socioeconomic factors, instead treating DNA samples as an opportunity to go gene hunting for continentally unique (what the media later reports as race-specific) disease variants. Researchers look at the various parts of an African American or Latinx person's DNA and then label disease variants of interest as "European" or "African" or "Native American." And once again we find genomic science advancing the notion that, at base, we are all distinct genetic races.

Good intentions abound in genomic science, and a complex understanding of what is at stake rules the field, whose leaders are committed to racial justice and to dispelling deterministic misinformation about race. However, good intentions are not enough. Complex understandings are also not enough. Scientists can "speak truth to power," as the political rallying cry says. But as long as genetic sampling and reporting are tagged to common racial categories, bracketing and therefore lacking sociopolitical analysis, we will continue to see race in terms of DNA differences.

CHAPTER 5

Genetics, IQ, and Behavior

▪   ▪   ▪   ▪   ▪   ▪   ▪

M Y INTERNAL STRUGGLE WITH THE contradictions around
what well-meaning genomic scientists believed was real about
race and worth studying led me to the emerging field of social and
behavioral genomics, "sociogenomics." In the last decade, many experts
researching intelligence, education, economics, and crime have conducted genomic studies in which they survey a person's genes to calculate a "risk score" for how intelligent they will likely be, how far they
might get in school, whether they will be aggressive or promiscuous or
perform violent acts—in other words, how "at-risk" they are to enact
specific social behaviors. Despite taking an antiracist stance in their
work in general and remaining agnostic about race in particular studies, some of these studies use highly racialized bodies of data, like IQ
averages, school statistics, and crime and sex rates, to build their algorithms, and many are conducted on the same racially classified DNA
samples that feed all genomic research. So, while many researchers
claim that their findings and risk scores pertain to "Europeans" or
"Asians" or "Africans" as genetic populations and not the social groups

we call races, analyses and reports are often inadvertently structured by race, risking the kind of misinterpretation that leads people to believe races have different mental abilities or behavioral tendencies.

Explaining behavior by the genetics of particular groups has proved perilous in the past. From some of the earliest characterizations of race, over 250 years ago, people have defined race in terms of differences in social behavior. Just recall Linnaeus's schematic with Asians and Africans as greedy and sly, and Europeans as wise and inventive, or Hume's claim that Europeans were the only race to possess the capacity to learn, so other races should be enslaved. Though all these thinkers' catalogs of purely physical traits—like skin color, height, and eye shape—were irrevocably harmful on their own, their conclusions about social and behavioral characteristics were the most corrosive part of their theory. The assumption that people's appearance reflected their inner value empowered the rational European—the one who claimed the capacity to know and see—to create and justify lies about minoritized "others."

Sociogenomic scientists reject these racist views and are extremely vocal and nuanced in their communications about the genetic groups they study. They are aware that their studies are uniquely vulnerable to genetic determinism around race, and they know that sociogenomics, with its dual emphasis on genes and the social environment, is well positioned to bring humanity original insights into the social reality of race. Despite holding summits to forge an antiracist path forward, thus far sociogenomics has not been able to outpace the demand for biased information around genetics, intelligence, and school achievement, nor have scientists been able to prevent misuses of data that align with racist policy. Nearly two decades into the field of research, scientists are still grappling with how to conduct genomic research that won't be used to perpetuate racism and bias.

A look at some major debates and policy disasters over the last seventy-five years can help us to understand what is going on today. Scientific discourses with unresolved racial biases are sometimes taken up in policymaking, which has attempted to promote antiracism by way of integration for some time. In *The Mismeasure of Minds*, historian Michael Staub showed that antiracist social and behavioral scientists have used racially biased genetics and IQ data to win many political battles from the post–World War II period to the present, including those that led to the desegregation of public education in the United States. During the infamous *Brown v. Board of Education* trial of the early 1950s, two different camps of social and behavioral science duked it out. One camp presented racial disparities in IQ scores, saying that scores proved the innate, intractable inequality of races. The other camp presented IQ scores to argue the opposite—that disparities in test scores showed that lower-scoring Black Americans needed to get the same education as higher-scoring White Americans to boost their cognitive performance. In the end, the US Supreme Court decided in favor of the integrationists. However, in hanging their arguments on IQ comparisons in DNA science and other emerging neurosciences, these promoters of antiracist policy unwittingly bolstered the legitimacy of sciences that confused nature with nurture and assumed clear genetic distinctions between racial groups.

Similarly, in the 1970s, educational psychologist Arthur Jensen's "How Much Can We Boost IQ and Scholastic Achievement?" set off a series of IQ debates involving behavior geneticists, psychologists, and evolutionary biologists. Whether promoting racism or antiracism, those on both sides of the debate rallied around the IQ test and the genetic science of the day to affirm the veracity of the tests even as they criticized Jensen's racist interpretations. As Aaron

Panofsky has shown in his in-depth look at the years that preceded and followed the IQ test controversy, behavioral geneticists rebuilt their field to appear both antiracist and scientifically robust using many of Jensen's approaches.

Soon after, in the mid-1990s, psychologist Richard Herrnstein and economist Charles Murray released *The Bell Curve*, an infamous book arguing that the fifteen-point IQ gap between Whites and Blacks, which intelligence experts called the "Racial Gap," was due to Blacks' inferior genetics. Many experts decried the book's racism, yet it sold tremendously. Once again, the international science community rallied around IQ science and used their own interpretations of the tests to provide an antiracist counterargument. To counter Herrnstein's and Murray's claim that the racial IQ gap was a result of genetics, the scientists retorted that the variation in average IQ was due to differences in opportunity, which could be improved with education. IQ tests and intelligence genetics were never criticized themselves. To the contrary, the international science community upheld the tests' legitimacy in a series of public statements.

Herrnstein passed away the year that *The Bell Curve* was published, but Murray has grown increasingly influential. He has maintained their original claim that racial minorities with low IQ scores are more likely to become criminals, commit violent crimes, behave promiscuously, and commit sex crimes, and he has carried this argument into contemporary debates, co-opting yesterday's social and behavioral genetics and today's social and behavioral genomics to support his points. In his most recent interviews he has said, "The violent crime rate among Blacks is ten times that what it is among whites . . . the same thing goes with differences in IQ." Murray claims that there is a genomic ceiling for Black people and that "entry into certain kinds of occupations is limited, because the cognitive demands of those occupations mean that a whole lot of more white people qualify than Black people."

Murray goes against the numerous studies that have shown that IQ is an inaccurate measure of intelligence. IQ tests do not measure brain activity or learning; rather they measure test performance. The fact that research shows that IQ scores have been rising worldwide along with improvements in living standards demonstrates that IQ is not determined by genetics, and instead is a product of social circumstances. Furthermore, IQ scores have risen significantly for members of all racial groups who are living in the most developed areas, especially in areas where public education is now available to all. This widespread increase in IQ illustrates the importance of equitable social systems like free and mandatory public schooling and shows how our IQ scores are not our genetic destiny, as Murray would have us believe.

Likewise, decades of studies into that "Racial Gap" in IQ scores that pundits like Murray love to harp on have revealed that score gaps have narrowed significantly in recent years. Furthermore, the rate at which Black Americans have raised their scores far surpasses the rate at which the general population's score has risen. If we believed that genetics were responsible for IQ scores, the sharp uptick would mean that Black people had evolved different brains and genomes from their parents and grandparents just in the last generation—an obviously ludicrous idea.

On the contrary, the rapid increase in the average IQ scores of Black Americans proves that there was never a time when human brains and genomes diverged into discrete and mutually exclusive forms. There are no fixed IQ averages for racial groups now and there never were.

Indeed, the trend only shows that the desegregation and racial equality measures of the past half century have raised Black American test performance.

MURRAY REPRESENTS A FACTION who believe themselves to be more legitimately antiracist than those who cry racism, because they provide "real talk" about the true nature of racial inequality. As he puts it, "certain kinds of outcomes exist that are not explained by racism, let alone systemic racism." Murray maintains that you can try to provide "better education, better nutrition, less poverty and the rest of it" but that racial inequality will persist because, in his view, the problem is in our genomes.

Murray's arguably hyper-racist, so-called realist stance dovetails with Genomic Race to produce a virulent form of racialism that even the most antiracist scientists have been powerless to overcome: the belief in *genomically* distinct and significant races. As Paul Gilroy said, racialism perpetuates the fictional existence of race even without a clear biological claim to hierarchy. So, while Murray's explicit language with a clear biological claim to hierarchy might alarm us, when we apply genomics to racial categories that are social in nature rather than biological, we too risk perpetuating genetic determinism and substantiating false notions of race.

Take, for example, the realm of economic policy. The left-leaning Urban Institute's guideline entitled "Genetics and Economic Mobility," published in 2008, tells policymakers that our genetics determine our socioeconomic status. Though the guideline is a well-meaning attempt to integrate the latest in genetic and social research, it asserts that "genetics play a role in intergenerational mobility," there is a "strong genetic link to cognitive skills," "a large portion of medical conditions have an underlying genetic component, implying that the inheritance of conditions that limit work may reduce intergenerational mobility," and there is a "link between genetics and antisocial behaviors that reduce individuals academic and labor market successes and economic mobility." In other words, the Urban Institute claims that our intelligence, health, and personality are genetically determined factors that can define our economic status. Though the guideline provides disclaimers saying that the jury is still out on the impact of genetic conditioning versus environmental conditioning, it bolsters the belief that the disparities in socioeconomic status and mobility among different racial groups stem at least in part from our genomes. Read alongside the statistics on racial wealth and income gaps, this essentially race-free tract implies scientifically bogus racial differences.

Genomic racialism also threatens to undermine another important policymaking realm—criminal justice. Leaders in the criminal justice system have turned to social and behavioral genomic studies to inform cases and policymaking in courts, in justice facilities, and on the streets. For over a decade, defense attorneys have been using social and behavioral genomic tests in trial litigation to argue that their clients were driven by their DNA to commit violent crimes. These attorneys have based their DNA evidence on tests looking for a so-called "aggression gene" during a flurry of social and behavioral gene hunts for criminal behaviors such as violence, rape, gang participation, and even defaulting on credit cards. While very few of these studies have made overtly racial claims—such as implying that criminal genes are the provenance of one minority group or another—media coverage of these tests has been highly racialized. In 2009, for example, *New Scientist* published "'Gangsta Gene' Identified in US Teens" alongside a photo of a Latinx gang.

Another less public and yet more insidious way that genomic racialism has played out in criminal justice is in policymaking around the incarcerated and those deemed criminally at-risk. In recent years, some experts have called for those working in justice facilities and other administrative, educational, and institutional domains to use genetic tests to identify potential threats and predict and prevent recidivism. They have done so despite the mass of research showing that racism, not genes, increases the likelihood that youth of color will be labeled "at-risk" by educators and subsequently policed, criminalized, institutionalized, and incarcerated. Some have even advocated for genetic testing of at-risk youth as early as possible, in infancy, so that caregivers and educators can identify antisocial tendencies, to turn youth from, in the words of one psychologist, "the path of violence."

These researchers have claimed that early intervention with genetically tailored anticrime programs can prevent a person's innate antisociality and criminality from expressing itself. Other researchers have called for genetic testing of at-risk adults, especially those who are already incarcerated or forcibly institutionalized. Some of the policy recommendations that have emerged from this supposedly race-agnostic research include testing prisoners to see what kinds of crimes or infractions they are "genetically vulnerable" to committing, determining the risk for recidivism in sentencing multi-offense convicts, deciding whether to release mental patients on suicide watch, or whether to permit people with post-traumatic stress disorder (PTSD) to own weapons. But crime is not a "gene." Both the tests and the policies that these behavioral risk scores are inspiring are wrongheaded. Applied to the systemically racist education, juvenile justice, and prison systems, genetic tests would only further disenfranchise the groups that these systems are stacked against.

People of color, especially Black male youth, are already disproportionately criminalized, policed, and brutalized in most countries in the world where genetically deterministic notions of race have been on the rise. In recent years, White Nationalism has resurged in mainstream politics. White supremacist discourse has spiked in the media. Far-right politicians running on genetically deterministic platforms have been elected to the highest executive offices in Asia, Australia, Europe, and North and South America. The punditry of genomic racialists like Murray, who advocate for racialized criminal justice systems, education, and occupations, has grown in popularity worldwide.

Law enforcement is already policing people of color with another racialist genomic technology: genetic facial recognition software known as DNA "photofits." Photofits take a forensic sample of a substance such as hair or saliva and construct an image of a suspect that law enforcement can then use in dragnets. As I and others who have visited photofit labs and studied the technology have found, its algorithms link specific facial features to OMB groups, thereby creating a racial readout for use in law enforcement and criminal justice. In other words, the technology assigns racial calculations of skin and hair color, eye and nose shape, and other facial characteristics to DNA samples and compels its users to racially profile based on its analyses. Photofits have been used in racialized DNA "dragnets"—stop-and-test procedures in which law enforcement set up DNA-testing checkpoints in an area where a suspect is thought to be. Everyone who fits the description is stopped and asked to provide a cheek swab regardless of their involvement in any crime. As in the case of IQ tests, the makers of the technology assure the public of its scientific merits, insisting that any problems are in the bias of its *application*, not its *algorithm*. Yet the biases are programmed deep within the technology. Today, even as new debates emerge around AI-based profiling and race, genetic facial recognition software remains ubiquitous, providing criminal justice with one of its most high-tech racialist technologies yet.

MANY SCIENTISTS WORKING ON sociogenomic research have been driven by an antiracist imperative in the field of education. When conducting the research for my book *Social by Nature* in the 2010s, I found that those who were spearheading the latest sociogenomic projects and consortia had spent their careers analyzing the relationship between race and educational outcomes, while others had conducted influential research debunking racist claims about IQ. Yet genomic racialism has flourished in the sometimes explicitly antiracist realm of education, where policymaking rooted in social and behavioral science about the heritability of intelligence, intellectual aptitude, and cognitive and learning ability has been having a renaissance. Studies meant to prevent racism and racialism have unwittingly promoted them by relying on racially biased data on intellectual and educational outcomes.

In the past decade, genomic science has zeroed in on social outcomes in intelligence testing and time spent learning at school. It has adapted genomic methods to behavior, and as a result, behavioral scientists in a range of fields—from psychology and sociology to political science and economics—have begun searching for genetic variants predictive of IQ scores (what they call "intelligence") and how far a student progresses in school (what they call "educational attainment"), as well as risk scores for low performance and academic deficiency. Intelligence studies claim to have found hundreds of genetic variants affecting thousands of genes at work in creating the foundational architecture of our brains. Some scientists believe these variants may one day be predictive of IQ test performance and intellectual ability from early childhood or even the womb. Similarly, some use educational attainment as a proxy for cognitive ability and brain health. Studies claim to have found almost 4,000 variants potentially affecting most of the genome, and that may one day be predictive of cognitive performance throughout life.

Many scientists responsible for these studies hope to find ways to identify people with, as some call it, "low intelligence" or "limited learning capacity," so caregivers and educators can help customize educational programs to meet a learner's unique needs. Many have progressive politics and, like the genomic scientists I have worked with over the years, they publicize their views on the importance of social equality. However, race is both nowhere and everywhere in this scientific effort. We know the science of intelligence is based on a racially stratified network of DNA samples. In fact, the latest educational attainment study was able to amass its three million DNA samples thanks to 23andMe's dataset, a collection intentionally cataloged according to "major ethnicities" that correspond to OMB's racial categories. Meanwhile, IQ rates, grade point average (GPA), and school attendance and completion rates are racially biased because the social and educational environments in which youth live are rife with structural racism. In Australia, for example, where Indigenous Australians earn incomes that are approximately half the incomes of all other Australians, less than 70 percent of all Indigenous Australians complete high school (with only about 40 percent from rural areas graduating), while over 90 percent of White Australians do. Indigenous Australians, likewise, make up less than 1 percent of the population of students who have obtained a PhD.

On the one hand, scientists in intelligence studies profess antiracist politics and warn that brain architecture and genetic ancestry are complicated, and that there is no direct correspondence between genetic ancestry and race. In interviews and op-eds, they repeatedly assert that they are not in the business of researching one race or the supposed racial IQ gap, and many criticize the notion of anyone doing so. As lead scientist Danielle Posthuma explained in *The New York Times*: "If you try to predict height using the genes we've identified in Europeans in Africans, you'd predict all Africans are five inches shorter than Europeans, which isn't true." The same goes for intelligence variants, she maintains, as any competent behavioral scientist would.

On the other hand, researchers try to avoid racialized comparisons by researching only one continental group—most often their own "European" group. But in researching one quasi-racial group like "Europeans," they are still making the implicit claim that continental descent is a stand-in for genetic ancestry. Just the act of demarcating "people of European descent"—as if genetic variation were continental and discrete as opposed to gradual and continuous—contributes to the false narrative that race is genetically real. So, though scientists discuss their choices in an antiracist manner, the use of racial categories at the heart of their studies results in racially stratified findings.

We can see how dangerous these unresolved contradictions about race and racialism are when we look at research applications in biotech and education. In biotech, several organizations have developed genetic intelligence tests and apps using a person's 23andMe or Ancestry.com data that they have purchased from one of the consumer genomics companies. In 2017, GenePlaza created the "Intelligence App," which applied 23andMe data to construct a genetic intelligence score and an educational attainment score for its customers. In 2018, DNA Land built an IQ "prediction engine" around intelligence studies specifically.

In 2022, Genomelink told customers that the "newly identified gene loci" in the third educational attainment study identified genes related to "neuron-to-neuron communication, which is how brain cells receive and send signals to each other," and promised customers that they could say to what extent their genes were "nudging you to stay in school."

These companies join the many DNA test-kit companies that have already been sequencing customers' DNA and creating reports on a litany of behavioral traits and characteristics. In recent years, as intelligence and educational attainment research has streamed in, these companies have stepped up their business of IQ prediction. Nowhere do test- and app makers explain the socially contingent, racialized nature of IQ scores or educational attainment rates. Instead, their "insights" arguably peddle racism's core belief—the scientifically false and socially harmful notion that your DNA code determines your aptitude.

Another looming threat with the application of sociogenomic research concerns "designer babies." Preimplantation Genetic Diagnosis, or PGD, is a reproductive procedure used with in vitro fertilization (IVF) that allows scientists to figure out whether an embryo has a specific disease risk so that a prospective parent can decide whether to implant a specific embryo and carry it to term. To date, PGD has been primarily used along with IVF to help couples with a high risk for a genetic disorder such as cystic fibrosis or Down syndrome to select a healthy embryo. However, as Steve Hsu of the biotech firm Genomic Prediction has said, the genomic pattern that predicts educational attainment can also predict IQ, and so companies can use that information to select for higher IQ embryos. Though PGD only contributes to a very small percentage of babies born around the world today, this technology is projected to grow in popularity as social and behavioral genomic risk scores and tests become more prevalent. Through the efforts of companies like Genomic Prediction, IVF-PGD could breed a pernicious eugenic form of Genomic Race, where parents choose babies that companies promise "avoid the risk" of low IQ.

Hsu also imagines a world in which prospective parents are empowered by the public health system to use gene-editing technologies like CRISPR to create hyperintelligent offspring. As he told RadioLab in 2019, "If I go out in the population and I look at people with [a low IQ] score, a lot of them have not had very, you know, I think, positive lives. And I'm pretty sure that most mothers, when they're pregnant, when they go to sleep at night, they're not dreaming about that outcome. They're dreaming about another outcome for their children." Hsu believes that prospective parents will one day be able to select embryos with IQs near 1,000 according to today's averages (ten times today's average score) using gene-editing technologies that don't require IVF, so, he argues, we will need a system that enables parents to avail themselves of the technology. Hsu laments the American public health system, which currently supports public sentiments of skepticism toward boosting intelligence and selecting for cognitive traits. To him this convention is Eurocentric—it's racist *not* to want hyperintelligent babies because it elides other cultures that he believes are eager to use technology to produce hyperintelligent offspring. Hsu believes that we need an antiracist retrofit of the current system to allow people to choose the children they want to have.

Hsu's "antiracist" dream of hyperintelligent babies exposes the racialist, if not racist, dangers of genomic interventions in policy. What Hsu doesn't say is how Black people and other minoritized people will fare given that they consistently receive low IQ scores relative to the White population because of persistent test biases that privilege White test takers. When society elevates one group and pushes the others down, the predictors across those groups reflect that same societal stratification. When the elevated group's scores predict the success of their offspring, the genomic risk scores reflect the privileged social treatment that they enjoyed. Will those who score low due to racial test biases be selected against and edited out of existence? Hsu's brave new health order would come with all the inherent biases yet no protections against this technologically advanced, stealthy form of eugenics (or "good breeding," as Francis Galton coined it so long ago). With algorithmic bias infiltrating more parts of society than ever, people of color would face a more high-tech threat than ever before.

Some parents may be uncomfortable selecting for intelligence pre-utero or in utero, but still may opt for schools structured by the latest sociogenomic research. Some education experts advocate restructuring entire education systems around genomic risk scores and tests, using the findings from the variants that they have published in their intelligence and learning research reports to guide a child through school. The most dominant voices among them support so-called "precision education," education tailored to an individual's DNA.

Intelligence geneticist Robert Plomin summarizes the philosophy behind precision education: "It can't be right for education to continue to ignore genetic influence, because it's far and away the most important source of individual differences." Plomin argues that education must be "preventative," so that children with low aptitudes and/or children at high risk for learning difficulties will avoid failure. "Children go to school, they fail, they get diagnosed, they're given special resources but by then it's too late. They've only ever experienced failure and it's like putting Humpty Dumpty back together. Once you have the genes, you could predict difficulties and hopefully prevent them." In other words, this scientist portrays children with learning difficulties and disabilities as fragile eggs and believes that education must fix the worst of a child's genetic failures.

Plomin, who was appointed Commander of the Order of the British Empire for his scientific contributions and was one of the top-cited scientists of the twentieth century, advocates change on two levels, individual and educational. For the individual, he envisions that every child will have a "learning chip," a personal genomic chip that is "a reliable genetic predictor" of that child's innate strengths and weaknesses. For the educational system, he imagines that schools would offer diverse subjects and extracurricular activities so that children can select the subjects or activities that best suit their alleged genetic aptitude.

Plomin opposes public-school and private-school systems, as well as charter schools that attempt to salvage broken public schools with more rigorous education programs for all their students. To Plomin, the academic life is simply not for everyone. Instead, he believes, teachers and administrators should learn genomics and genomic prediction so that programs can track students to cultivate their utterly unique talents, even if that means a curriculum customized to nonacademic talents. Yet as revolutionary as genetically tailored education sounds, it would only widen the racial education gaps that already exist. White students who are already privileged by the education system's racialized environments would now have a "genetic" leg up with their risk scores.

Another prominent learning researcher, Kathryn Paige Harden, popularizes the idea of using risk scores for students so that schools can identify children who are particularly vulnerable to falling through the cracks. In her book *The Genetic Lottery* Harden argues that education in its current form unfairly rewards the "genetically endowed," because it fails to help those who are "genetically less fit." As she sees it, human intelligence is about luck; some people win the genomic jackpot, while others lose. Like Plomin, Harden argues that every student could thrive if provided with the right education—the education that meets the needs of their unique DNA.

Despite overlapping in many ways with Murray's and Plomin's more racialist and politically conservative messages, Harden outlines a policy framework that resonates with liberals who want to reinvest in our public-school systems. She suggests policymakers arm public school administrators and teachers with a student's genomic data to identify at-risk students and to rescue students who are headed for a fall with special academic programs. According to Harden, far from giving up on the academic needs of low-intelligence children, this policy would give them extra tutoring in the areas where they most need help.

Still, like Murray, Plomin, Hsu, and the many other scientists and experts who believe that genetically tailored policy is the answer, Harden's focus on so-called genomic disadvantage diverts our attention from the true problem: racism plaguing education. "Common intuitions about the scale of inequality in our society, and our imaginations about how much progress we would make if we eliminated the visible inequalities by race and class, are profoundly wrong," says Harden. "I'm not looking for a school that's going to treat all of my kids the same. I'm looking for a school that's going to equalize their ability to profit from that school, to learn, to accommodate their uniqueness." Indeed, Harden warns that schools that fail to "accommodate that role of chance and luck," and that run with a false hope of equality based on merit, will only push the "genetically downtrodden" further into turmoil. Harden says nothing about the racial bias built into the algorithms that measure intelligence and educational attainment, nor how these systemic overhauls will affect the *racially* downtrodden.

It is impossible to test for learning potential. Branding a student as a "slower learner" based on the student's genetics merely perpetu-ates the misunderstanding that learning potential is innate. Such policy overlooks the social-emotional factors shaped by racism and bias that are the largest contributors to a student's success. Students of color face barriers to their success that have nothing to do with their genetics. For example, students of color face teacher biases, such as being punished more harshly than their White classmates. They may also incur "stereo-type threat," or the anxiety that if they perform badly, they might con-firm a negative stereotype about their social group. Bias can even trail students of color when they succeed. Some may experience imposter syndrome and doubt their achievements.

Some advocates of genetically tailored education claim to be only making policy recommendations for "people of European descent," painting the scores and data they use as sacrosanct scientific truths. But in doing so, they ignore the mountains of research that show IQ tests and school environments *are* racially biased, and that there are racial inequalities confounding their data at every turn. Fur-thermore, these policies dovetail with the White supremacist myth that genetics drive educational outcomes, rather than inequalities by race and class. Social sciences and genomics, on the other hand, have shown that structural racism and bias drive school success, not innate genetics.

Policy schemes like these bespeak a dangerous form of eugenics, one in which purportedly race-free science could encode institutionalized genocide against people who are categorized as low-IQ. If education policy is implemented to select against people with low IQs, score gaps will widen. And as risk scores are refined, a low IQ score will become the marker of genetic failure. When minoritized people who have genetics associated with low scores are registered as losers, their DNA will be seen as innately inferior. And when the risk scores and DNA tests are extended beyond "Europeans," we could see a distortion of Hsu's vision in which genetic lineages of those who have faced racial biases (that is, low-scoring people of color) are removed from academic learning environments, selected against in IVF-PGD, and possibly even edited out of existence with CRISPR. In a nightmarish version of Harden's plan, students would be sorted into special-needs programs or schools based on their race. Or, even more terrifying, students of color would receive nonacademic training while White kids are shuttled off to elite schools. Because intelligence tests are biased in favor of the socially privileged and tend to confer higher scores on White test takers, we could even see the emergence of separate school systems for students sorted by "intelligence" and a return to racially "separate but *un*equal" education. Of course, these scenarios have historical precedents.

If we uncritically apply genomic data to our social world, compounded with the systemic biases of genomic economic and criminal policy, we could produce a reality where every institution is stratified based on a genomic interpretation of race. Genomics could lead us toward an intransigent "life by DNA," replacing all other knowledge bases and sociopolitical awarenesses of the social reality of race.

Holding genomics as the arbiter of race will always be inadequate to dismantling racism. All too often genetic science keeps our focus on physiological matters that are bracketed from the sociopolitical processes that perpetuate racism. As sociologist Oliver Rollins has shown in his research into contemporary criminological metrics, a "violent brain model" has become more popular in criminology in recent decades. This model, which combines brain scans with psychological test results to produce risk profiles, has enabled criminal justice experts and the scientific community alike to ignore the mountains of research proving how systemic racism and predatory policing drive racist incarceration and criminalization rates. Genomic differences don't funnel people of color into the criminal justice system, racism does. Research steeped in genomic models will only reinforce the belief that our genome impacts our behavior more than inequality.

Sociological analysis of more recent data models in educational psychology has similarly shown that novel analyses of neural processes threaten to eclipse analyses of social-structural factors of race, such as unfair hiring, housing, and basic schooling. In fact, many antiracist educational psychologists have framed racism's harms as a matter of undue emotional stress—that is, hurt feelings—and have sidestepped analysis of sociopolitical structures. Racism doesn't just hurt our feelings. It determines our health and life chances. The neuroscientific turn in educational psychology has, therefore, increased scientific and public awareness of genetics while decreasing our awareness of the social reality of racial inequality.

From *Brown v. Board of Education* to now, the onus has been on antiracist social and behavioral science to disavow IQ scoring, DNA testing, and genomic algorithms based on racially biased data. It may seem like contemporary science and policymaking are avoiding racial terms. In recent years, explicit references to race have been expunged from many economic, educational, and criminal justice policy proposals, replaced with coded words like "urban" versus "suburban," or "middle-class" versus "inner-city poor." Yet with race baked into its algorithms, impelling racialist applications and racist uses, we still face a world of tests, technology, and policy paradigms that risk perpetuating racism and bias. This pattern suggests that even race-neutral science, or science that is absent any mention of race, can be applied in ways that unconsciously proliferate racism.

CHAPTER 6

Making a Business of Race

OUR DESIRE TO CONNECT OUR behavior to our genetics has paved the way for a new market to emerge. Businesses understand our obsession with genetics and race and are profiting from it. They know none of us want to be "low IQ" or genetically disadvantaged, so they create easy-access products and services that can affirm the narratives we already tell about ourselves and others.

Today, a direct-to-consumer market in personalized medicine is booming thanks to DNA kits that sell people a racial view of their genes. Customers can open up an ancestry kit, swab their mouths, and get a readout of their genetic origins in Europe, Africa, Asia, or the Americas. The readouts often report which parts of their genomes correspond to these differing continental origins, which can correspond to the customer's self-identified race.

These same at-home DNA tests tell you about your predisposition to disease. When taken in tandem, the results of the race test and the health test can be mistakenly correlated. A slew of genetic medical reports depict diseases as belonging to certain racial groups.

Some examples are rare diseases like Tay-Sachs (more prevalent in the Amish, Ashkenazi Jews, Cajuns, and French Canadians but described in global media as a "Jewish disease"), sickle cell disease (more prevalent in Congolese, non-Hindi-speaking groups in India, and Nigerians, but described as a "Black disease"), as well as common diseases like hypertension (more prevalent in Filipinos and Indians of northeastern India, but described as a "Black disease"). While these afflictions do affect some people who share genetic ancestry, they do not affect most members of a given group, let alone all members of their race. In the Philippines, where there are over 170 different ethnic groups, those with the highest rates of hypertension are low-income city dwellers who smoke. In India, by contrast, those with the highest rates of hypertension are high-income city dwellers who eat expensive processed foods. The misconception that hypertension is a "Black disease" comes from its prevalence in the Western Hemisphere in African American and Afro-Latinx groups, who are more likely to live in poverty and lack access to high-quality food and medicine due to systemic racism, but disease rates within those groups are starkly different for people who enjoy health and wealth and those who do not.

Despite how medical tests are framed, those who suffer from diseases do not solely belong to one race or another. Hypertension is not most prevalent in or restricted to all people in Asia. Nor is it most prevalent in and restricted to all people of Asian descent. It is certainly not most prevalent in or restricted to people of African descent, as the Western myth of hypertension being a "Black disease" falsely claims. Diseases should never be construed as the property of a racial group.

Only diseases that are what scientists call "monogenic" (where having a specific gene means that you have a very high chance of getting a disease—Tay-Sachs, for example) are caused by a specific gene variant that can be traced to a genetic ancestral lineage. Through cultural practices of endogamy, or intermarriage within one community, these diseases have become more prevalent in specific groups (like the Amish and Ashkenazi Jews). And yet we still must not construe diseases as the property of one ethnic group or another, because ethnicity isn't simply genetics. As we know from the analyses of haplogroups, very different groups can share the same traits. Despite this, "racial medicines"—diagnoses and drugs that doctors only prescribe to one or another race—have begun to proliferate.

The reach of Genomic Race and its unique brand of racialism extend far beyond the academy to the private sector. In fact, most people will never take part in public DNA sampling. Rather, they will encounter genetic science via an ancestry test or a workup at their doctor's office.

Race has become a hot-ticket marketing trope that companies use to drive consumption. Genetic testing is a case in point. Though most direct-to-consumer tests do not report by race but rather by haplogroups or ancestral populations derived from proprietary DNA collections, their algorithms interpret DNA by race. Some companies even paint test results in quasi-racial terms that fuel the notion that there are different genetic races that DNA belongs to, so they can couch their reporting in popular narratives that resonate with test takers even when they know full well that a genetic test can't tell a person's race. The company 23andMe, for example, markets its ancestry tests to African Americans using branding from the History Channel's adaptation of Alex Haley's *Roots*.

Similarly, Big Pharma can repurpose a drug and create a new race-based market for it when developers see that the drug benefits a subgroup of a clinical-trial population based on samples taken from people who identify with the same race. Drug companies do this even if they have no genetic data on those participants showing that they share ancestry. Once a drug is approved as a racial medicine, companies influence healthcare providers to prescribe it based on patients' self-identified race or the race that doctors believe a patient to be. This practice introduces a form of genomic racialism that conforms to systemic racism in the private sector, health and medicine, and beyond.

Where did the market in genetic testing and race-based medicine arise, I wondered, when I first visited a test maker, 23andMe, in 2008. Genealogy has long been a national pastime in countries with rich multicultural heritages, but in the early 2000s a cottage industry in DNA testing cropped up in the United States and the United Kingdom offering people a chance to unlock their past on a genetic level. That small industry has since risen to become a multibillion-dollar market. Testing kits that once cost in the thousands now cost less than a hundred dollars. As its accessibility has grown, genetic genealogy, with a market estimated to reach $20 billion in 2024, has eclipsed historical genealogy, a $4 billion industry.

Direct-to-consumer genetic testing didn't always deal in race. It started out as a business of haplogroup reporting based on the knowledge emerging from international genome projects like the Human Genome Project and HapMap. Companies with names like GeneTree and Family Tree DNA drew Y-chromosome DNA and mtDNA (the DNA that exists outside of the cell's nucleus, in the mitochondria) from customer blood samples. They then mapped customers' haplotypes and confirmed that they belonged to specific haplogroups, often giving a certificate of membership to the "I1" "Nordic" group or the "L1" "Central and West Africa" group.

But things soon changed when the National Geographic Society began offering direct-to-consumer ancestry kits in an effort to conduct its own international genome project, the Genographic Project.

Though this aimed to create a collection of DNA from close-knit human populations as opposed to broad continental populations, the project marketed itself as capturing the DNA of people who could be used as a proxy for Old World continental groups—groups that existed before colonialism and globalization. In its outreach materials the Genographic Project showed an image of a person from each continent, depicting the false narrative that there were original continental populations and original DNA lineages that corresponded to race.

At this point, companies began promising to link consumers' DNA to "genetic cousins" on distant continents in a show of racial relatedness. Many new companies emerged with the explicit goal of uncovering people's racial roots and diasporic belonging according to hidden lineages in their DNA. Companies with names like "Roots for Real" and "African Ancestry," for example, claimed they could link British and American nationals to specific countries on the African subcontinent by mapping their haplotypes, even though company scientists knew that those haplotypes were shared by people living all over the world. Companies held out a link to a much-desired homeland for Black people, knowing that colonizers and slave traders had sought to erase African ties during enslavement. These companies erroneously implied that a person's genetic cousins were real cousins to them, and that those family members originated in the exact spot where they had been sampled—as if people from Cameroon and Namibia have had similar genetic makeups throughout time. These companies not only reinforced the notion that race was a matter of genetics but also masked the reality of human migrations across and between continents, migrations that have been taking place since humans first traveled from and returned to Africa over 60,000 years ago.

Other companies, like DNAPrint Genomics, made even shoddier

racial claims. DNAPrint used genomic software to map customers' DNA to continental groups—what they and other developers referred to as "admixture mapping." Though these companies looked at only about 150 of the over three billion genetic variants in a person's genome to produce test results, they assigned continental labels to these few variants and then apportioned people's genomes by race. So, even though the companies acknowledged the admixed nature of their customers point blank, they returned DNA to consumers with pie chart reports claiming that their DNA lineages were best interpreted by race.

This method of reporting genomics by race has been particularly damaging in the case of companies like 23andMe, who calls its admixture-mapping "chromosome painting," which breaks down a customer's chromosomes into Old World quasi-racial groups. Companies, including 23andMe, have simultaneously launched direct-to-consumer medical testing by race. In advance of generating a readout of the carrier status of the specific gene variants that the customer possesses for cancer, dementia, wellness, or metabolism, 23andMe classifies consumers by "major ethnicity," or their main continental affiliation, implicating race in its basic algorithm. The algorithm then generates the customers' risks by reading their DNA against a racial subset of the medical literature instead of interpreting their genetic risks based on their ancestral haplotypic code.

Companies have displayed racialism as they have played upon racial stereotypes around physical, mental, and intellectual fitness. Genetic Performance, a maker of sports ability tests, has depicted Whites swimming versus Blacks slam-dunking in their marketing materials and on their website. Warrior Roots, a maker of aggression tests, has depicted lighter-skinned Vikings alongside darker-skinned modern soldiers. The Makings of Me, a maker of IQ and talent tests, has depicted Asian kids playing violin and White kids exploring with a microscope. Sadly, these racial tropes aren't just marketing ploys. Companies coax consumers to live to their "potential" by implying that they should choose a career or select a hobby based on the results of their test, as if living to one's potential is living up to one's genetic race.

Companies argue that they provide enough information in their FAQs and disclaimers to stave off the spread of inaccurate racial assumptions. However, consumer research has shown that there is much more going on. Studies conducted on consumers from different backgrounds consistently indicate that consumers seek to confirm or affirm specific identities that they find desirable precisely *because* they correspond to positive racial stereotypes or contradict negative ones.

Some of the well-meaning attempts to use genetic technology to improve lives involve people with Native American heritage. Native Americans, or those claiming Native heritage, may use genetic ancestry tests to substantiate their own racial membership so that they can access the rights and resources afforded members of that group. At face value, this seems an innocuous use of genomic technology because it could help people affirm their membership in a group that claims them. But policy analyst Kim TallBear, a member of the Sisseton Wahpeton Oyate nation in South Dakota, has described how definitions of kinship are changing for the worse in this era of genetic ancestry testing.

Recall that in the past Indigenous Americans took proof of belonging from those who were born in the tribal community to tribal members. Now there are dozens of companies, like DNA Consultants with its "Basic American Indian DNA Test," that peddle tests to Native Americans to use as proof of their identity. A study conducted by NIH researchers Hina Walajahi, David Wilson, and Sara Hull in 2019 found that approximately one third of all DNA testing companies were selling kits to test for Native American ancestry as a distinct category. Of these companies, only three attempted to distinguish between genetic ancestry and race.

As Genelux, a company TallBear has exposed, has advertised: "Whether your goal is to assist in validating your eligibility for government entitlements such as Native American Rights or just to satisfy your curiosity, our Ancestry DNA test is the only scientifically rigorous method available for this purpose in existence today." Genelux and other companies target Native Americans through newsletters and online forums to sell them a new form of proof of their membership that can help them bypass former requirements. And this niche marketing is particularly racializing because it wholly displaces the category of tribal membership (membership in a specific tribe) in favor of racial membership (having Native American ancestry). As we know, tests cannot establish or substantiate genetic ties to specific tribes with any certainty. DNA can only establish the probability of a correspondence to haplogroups in the Americas—that is, continental, quasi-racial, American membership.

TallBear also describes how in recent years some tribal leaders have begun using genetic ancestry testing to root out claimants who have an insufficient amount of indigenous ancestry. Complicated by the litany of racial appropriations by Whites attempting to gain tribal membership to revamp their racial identities and/or access tribal wealth, some tribes have decided to use testing to their benefit. Yet, adopting this technology can be extremely contentious because relying on genetics can weaken a tribe's prior system for using tribal ties to determine membership. Investing in scientific methods to define belonging can devalue a group's autonomy in defining kinship for themselves.

Another case of genetic testing that appropriates racial identity concerns companies that advertise to AfroBritish, AfroCanadian, AfroCaribbean, and African American "root-seekers" who are pursuing genetic confirmation of their African origins. Companies sell their products with images of ancient civilizations as depicted in heroic epics. Alondra Nelson has revealed how companies profit from legacies of racial oppression, robbing descendants of formerly enslaved communities of truly knowing their homeland by selling them an "undifferentiated racial identity" as Black. Nelson reminds us that genetic ancestry tests cannot identify real ties to real people. Nor can they identify any ties to real tribes.

Nelson warns that genetic claims-making, or establishing legitimacy by genomics, could fast eclipse historical and cultural claims-making, or establishing legitimacy by historical records. Her analysis of Kittles's company, African Ancestry, shows that tests are rapidly gaining official status as they make their way from bedside to bench—from the privacy of people's homes to the publicity of courtroom battles. Nelson established that by the early 2000s, African Ancestry had disseminated upward of 100,000 "Certificates of Ancestry" to people of African descent interested in proving their ties to Africa. In 2005, African Ancestry provided legal vouchers for plaintiffs seeking reparations for slavery, claiming that their genetic ancestry established them as descendants of the enslaved. Despite the eventual dismissal of the case, the US courts set a precedent by permitting genetic tests to be admitted as evidence of racial membership. Tests have since been elevated beyond their original "recreational" intent to a status of forensic evidence pertinent to race-based litigation.

Following these events closely reveals that the real danger of the racialist application of genomics is in allowing genetic membership to overshadow, or potentially eliminate, participatory membership in spe-

cific racial groups. In the past, family membership, community participation, social identification, and political action have been the basis of
racial membership. What happens when the true mark of belonging is
an ancestry test, rather than participation and reciprocity?

Genetic test results tell us nothing about our real social ties or experiences. They say nothing about our struggles to empower our communities. Race is a social reality that should not be misinterpreted through
genetic testing. Ignoring the social realities of race, genetic test results
make race seem to be just a matter of our DNA. As such, they invalidate those very ties and experiences that have led us to be identified a
certain way and to have suffered a certain way.

AT ITS CORE, RACIALISM is dangerous because it enables us to
uphold positive stereotypes about different races while leaving the belief
in fundamental racial differences intact. Because our social systems are
already biased toward racist algorithms, any core belief that we are part
of essentially different groups will perpetuate racism. *Genomic* racialism is even more "essentializing" because it affirms positive stereotypes
while implying that there are *genomically* distinct racial groups worth
baking into those algorithms. Genomic racialism is particularly insidious when mobilized in marketing schemes and sold to the public as
technological salves for our sociopolitical quandaries.

Law professor and sociologist Dorothy Roberts sees genomic racialism and direct-to-consumer "next-generation" genomics marketing as a
"fatal invention," a technology of oppression being innovatively weap-
onized against people of color. She draws our attention to how race is
consistently reborn in the latest biotech innovations, innovations that
displace other ways of belonging to or claiming group status. As these
technologies compel the racially privileged and the racially oppressed

alike to validate themselves by their algorithms, the innovations invalidate prior communal senses of race and politics while lending an imprimatur of material reality to high-tech constructions.

This never-ending upcycling of race via tech is particularly "fatal" to citizenship because it makes citizenship a matter of innate biology and not political participation. By allowing DNA readouts to serve as gateways to rights and resources, governments enable citizens to ignore the sociopolitical experiences that racially stratify access to healthcare, housing, education, and safety. Structural racism determines our life experiences and opportunities, not DNA. By taking stock in genetic tests, governing bodies deprioritize those political experiences, thereby ensuring that second-class citizenship will never truly be abolished.

Roberts's words about the fatal invention of race prove sage when we consider the uptake of genetic ancestry tests in the White supremacist community, a trend that has skyrocketed in the past decade, as evidenced by the numerous posts on genetic-testing forums hosted by 23andMe as well as alt-right and White Nationalist forums like Stormfront.org, 4chan's "politically incorrect" /pol/board, and reddit's /r/WhiteRights, /r/DebateAltRight, and /r/AltRight boards. By 2016, threads about genetic ancestry testing for Whiteness, and White Nationalism in particular, were appearing many times a week on these forums. As one journalist wrote: "This loose group of mostly young white men are tech- and media-savvy and not particularly religious, oppose immigration, and may support more extreme steps to make America whiter, such as repealing the 14th Amendment, which guarantees birthright citizenship. They often feel like it's a thoughtcrime to take pride in white identity, and they want a safe space to celebrate it." Testing for Whiteness has rapidly become a badge of honor for White

Nationalists, as well as a means of staking out White space and issuing alt-right doctrine.

In this case of genomic racialism, people with European heritage use tests, against company recommendations, to prove their Whiteness so that they can legitimize their sense of worth and privilege. They revel in test results that corroborate their racial superiority and use them to draw imagined boundaries, such as the genetic limits between the White race and others. They also use their test results to claim genes associated with advantageous traits, such as high IQ or mental fortitude. They even use tests to inspire political action, such as generating a kind of genetic passport ID card for White supremacists and a citizenship verifier to all outside their community. As Roberts suggests, this latest incarnation of genetic race allows White supremacists to go beyond racist antagonism and devise original avenues of doctrine and practice.

One trend is the use of ancestry tests by White supremacists to challenge supposed liberal lies—specifically the notion that all humans are related and descended from a common African ancestor, and that we are all, therefore, of "mixed" ancestry. White supremacists are particularly drawn to 23andMe's ancestry estimation service because it gives them a quasi-racial percentage report, such as "99.7% European." White supremacist test takers co-opt this ancestry estimation to assert their purity and prove the genetic robustness of the European category. Some have appropriated genetic concepts as well, for example, co-opting the concept of routine "statistical error" to claim that slight biases in test results are normal, so majority-European tests must be interpreted as 100 percent White.

Another White supremacist trend is to use ancestry tests to concoct supposedly scientific explanations for the fact that White people have a wide range of skin tones, hair colors, hair texture, and facial features. White supremacists discuss how it is their duty to post their "ethnic" breakdown to show that they hail from pure European lineages that include darker hair and eye color. They distinguish White ethnic mixture from the mixture of what they call "mud people," or the "mongrel hordes" of "non-White" people of color. In so doing, they put a new, modern spin on the old notion of purity as continental.*

An even more disturbing trend, however, is White supremacists' use of genetic ancestry tests for xenophobic, eugenic purposes. As noted, test taking among White supremacists is chiefly celebratory and associated with "positive" eugenics—proving a person's Whiteness so that they can procreate and spread "good genes" in the world. However, analysts have also seen the opposite—a "negative" form of eugenics where White supremacists pressure members of the community to use test takers' non-European test results to identify people to denounce, harass, or kill. As one test taker put it: "As a member of the alt-right you have to DNA test all of your friends and if they're not 100% White then you report them to your local Atomwaffen [neo-Nazi terrorist organization]." Other White supremacists have argued that their members must utilize the full suite of genetic technologies to "breed out

---

* Aaron Panofsky and Joan Donovan have analyzed what Stormfront White Nationalists do when they receive a mixed ancestry test result that suggests membership in an unwanted racial or ethnic group such as Jewish or Black. Finding several patterns emerging, including but not limited to discounting the validity of particular tests, they argue for the use of historical genealogy instead and denounce certain companies as being controlled by Jews.

non-white ancestry," for example, pairing test results with "preimplantation genetic testing," forced abortion, and the like.

IF THESE USES OF test results weren't disturbing enough, a second arm of the ancestry market more directly tethers race to genetics, producing an unshakable form of genomic racialism: race-based medicine. Race-based medicine is the bevy of drugs and diagnostics designed for use in specific races. While race-based medicine is less flagrantly racist than the use of ancestry tests by White supremacists, it is nonetheless pervasive and harmful.

BiDil, the first race-based medicine, was approved by the FDA in 2005 for use in Black people only. The drug, which combined two generic vasodilators in one pill to reduce the "pill burden" of those taking both, was initially developed for anyone at risk of heart failure. But when the FDA denied its approval because the combined pill did not prove more efficacious than the two generics taken together, BiDil's makers turned to race-based data to salvage the drug.

They argued that in trials the very small subset of subjects who self-identified as Black or African American showed substantial improvement, so they obtained a new patent from the US Patent Office and commissioned a study in which they administered the drug only to people who identified as Black. BiDil's makers also partnered with and got funding from high-profile Black associations, such as the NAACP, Congressional Black Caucus, Association of Black Cardiologists, and the National Medical Association. Together, they launched a national marketing campaign that painted race-based medicine as a political right.

In 2005, the drug's makers abruptly ended all trials and petitioned the FDA for approval of their "Blacks only" drug. The FDA then held a hearing in which many critics revealed the reported inadequacies of the drug's development. First, none of the study participants' DNA was sampled or analyzed in any of the trials, so there existed no proof that study participants who self-identified one way or another shared substantial genetic ancestry or had ancestry in common with otherwise-identified participants.

Second, the first trial did not prove greater efficacy in Black people, because few Black people were included in the trial. Instead, the numbers were likely a statistical artifact, one that was useful for the drug's makers in gaining a new lease on their patent.

Third, and most troubling, a second trial had no control group to prove that there was greater efficacy in people of African descent. There was no "non-Black" or "non–African American" control group. Instead, BiDil's makers created a media campaign claiming that people of African descent were genetically predisposed to heart disease.

At the FDA hearing, genetic epidemiologists presented counter-evidence showing that across the world, "White" Danes and Germans had the highest rates of heart disease, while "Black" Nigerians had the lowest. Furthermore, White Americans and African Americans fell somewhere in the middle of the spectrum of prevalence of heart disease, though African Americans fell closer on the spectrum to the Danes and Germans. In other words, shared African ancestry played less of a role in disease disparities than shared environment.

Despite the lack of evidence that BiDil was more efficacious in people of African descent, the FDA approved the drug. This decision opened a new avenue in drug development in which drug makers with failing patents and approvals could "rescue" their drugs by repurposing them as more effective for a select racial group.

In the months leading up to BiDil's approval, genome scientists noted at least twenty-nine drug applications in the US pipeline that claimed racial specificity. Some notable examples that gained a leg up include AstraZeneca's lung cancer drug Iressa, which repurposed itself as an "Asian" drug and similarly rescued the pharmaceutical company from the loss of billions in drug-development funding. The Iressa trial also generated no genetic data on its participants, but rather used self-identified race as a proxy for genetic ancestry.

Forest Laboratories' Bystolic, a cardiovascular drug designed for hypertension, was rebranded as a "Mexican" drug. Forest Laboratories would go on to market it as a better beta-blocker for Black people, spinning its own tales of the genetic dangers that beta-blockers posed to people of African descent.

A number of drugs and diagnostics have also framed themselves as racial without support by the Patent Office or FDA approval. For example, spirometers that determine lung function require healthcare providers to enter the race of a given patient so the machine can calibrate its data to OMB-based standards. The makers of blood thinners like warfarin and statins like Crestor instruct providers to prescribe the drug differently based on a patient's race, claiming that different races have different coagulation genetics. These drugs and diagnostics benefit from being perceived as race-friendly and of resisting the label of "colorblind" or "Eurocentric" even as they perpetuate harm to the very groups they claim to help.

RACE-BASED DRUGS REQUIRE THAT doctors and patients imaginatively connect the dots between racial identity and the utility of a given therapy in the absence of genetic analysis. The danger lies in these medicines' vast sphere of influence. They don't simply affect bench scientists who work with racially categorized DNA collections or consumers who opt to take an ancestry test. The influence of these drugs extends beyond the halls of science, and beyond people's private homes, to our public institutions of medicine and healthcare. There they become a foundation for diagnosis and prevention, patient–provider relations, and patient care.

The idea that races have their own diseases, traits, and risks already infiltrates health and medicine by way of clinical genetic testing. When a couple considers having a child, doctors often suggest that each individual take a genetic test to determine whether they possess unhealthy, disease-associated genetic variants that could put a fetus or a baby at risk if found in both parents. At present, these tests are structured by race into what providers refer to as "African" panels, "Caucasian" panels, and "Asian" panels.* Furthermore, when one member of a couple is already pregnant, doctors often work with genetic counselors to urge use of these panels as part of prenatal screening.

Hospitals and other medical facilities have their own risk-management policies that supersede a provider's own sense of best practices. For example, Boston Medical Center, the largest safety-net hospital in New England, lists genetic-risk factors in terms of seven "ethnicities," four of which correspond to races. Kaiser Permanente, the largest managed care organization in the United States, lists four genetic-risk-carrier groups, three of which correspond to races.

Even without genetic technologies at hand, medicine and healthcare are already riddled with racial biases. Clinical research shows that race-based language not only pervades diagnosis, treatment, and decision making via clinical algorithms and guidelines like the ones just

---

* Some researchers separate Ashkenazi Jewish and French-Canadian risk variants into their own panels.

described, but also via healthcare providers' individual biases and stereotypes about what groups have what diseases. The American Heart Association, for example, gives patients a Heart Failure Risk Score by assigning three fewer points to any patient identified as Black. Similarly, the National Kidney Foundation's kidney failure prediction algorithms assign higher estimated glomerular filtration rate (eGFR) values for anyone identified as Black. Doctors implement and comply with these algorithms and guidelines because they believe it is for the good of the patient. They're marking people as potential risks so that they can receive treatment, but there are clearly issues with offering blanket treatments for everyone with the same skin tone or perceived race.

In general, implicit bias tests reveal that providers hold positive attitudes for White patients and negative attitudes for people of color. Providers also tend to view Black and Latinx patients with suspicion and, at times, derision, seeing Blacks as noncooperative drug seekers and Latinx as noncompliant risk takers. The latest systematic reviews of studies across the field show that racial biases are rampant in medicine and healthcare.

Analyses of medical education reveal that training materials and practice paradigms conflate genetic ancestry and race, teach racial disease stereotyping, and encourage the use of racial shortcuts in diagnosis and care. Systems and programs even instruct future healthcare providers to prescribe drugs based on a patient's race using a number of national and international treatment standards, such as guidelines provided by the US Joint National Committee and the FDA. So, it comes as no surprise that downstream analyses of treatment confirm that Whites receive the gold standard of care while people of color, especially Black people, receive substandard care, especially regarding patient–provider interactions and treatment decisions. From rare conditions like spinal cord injuries to common ones like stroke, people of color are repeatedly assigned subpar treatments on the market. Even psychological diseases like anorexia or major depression are less likely to be diagnosed (and subsequently treated) for people of color, especially Black people. This inequity leads people of color to suffer declining health and poorer health outcomes, often fatal.*

When companies send the message that race is a proxy for genetic populations and that races have their own unique genetic risks, it creates a false belief in the genetic reality of race while detracting from its social reality. It constructs race as genomic fact rather than social reality. To address this, the government could ban racial drugs and mandate that the companies behind these technologies and therapies use clear, distinctive language to communicate the true meaning of DNA test results and medicines. Consumer and patient advocacy groups could monitor companies as they inform providers and patients about alternative algorithms to race. Retaining the paradigm of Genomic Race will only preserve bias and bring us to an even deeper, intractable separate and unequal state of affairs in healthcare, medicine, and beyond.

---

* Consider three areas for which stark treatment biases exist: hypertension, chronic pain, and mental illness. In the first case, providers have been shown to prescribe Blacks different medications than Whites and provide poorer disease management, hastening illness. In the second, providers have been shown to prescribe Blacks different medications, often refusing care entirely, leading to worsening symptoms and more frequent disease crises. In the third, providers have been shown to treat Whites with antidepressants and therapy while refusing treatment to people of color. In the case of mentally ill youth, providers have been shown to disproportionately turn patients of color over to penal services; in the case of mentally ill adults, they disproportionately recommend patients of color for incarceration.

CHAPTER 7

Deconstructing Race

■ ■ ■ ■ ■ ■ ■

I S IT POSSIBLE FOR GENETIC science to make a contribution regarding the reality of race that doesn't reinforce genetically deterministic thinking? Does any form of racialism—the belief that there are significant racial differences—belong in science? These questions continue to haunt the minds of many people working in and around genomics and those who, like me, want to know how racism stratifies our health. Precisely because race is a reality, we need new models of scientific study that elicit a greater understanding of how that reality is evolving, especially how it becomes real for our health, and thus our life chances.

In my research, I have found that there are responsible ways to use race in science and there are kinds of science that are making a positive difference to racism. A current subfield of genetics analyzes how our social environments dictate what our DNA can do. That field is epigenetics.

Until recently, scientists believed that DNA alone was responsible for the cellular differentiations and protein production that make humans into the unique beings that we are. But today they have homed in on the molecules that provide the granular instructions for our DNA machinery: our epigenome (the prefix "epi" is derived from the Greek word for "atop"). The epigenetic markers that make up our epigenome bind to our DNA and manipulate it to turn on or off. These markers "regulate," or direct, our DNA to make which proteins when.

Some people have likened the epigenome to our body's instruction manual. Others compare it to an orchestra that plays our DNA sheet music or the software for our DNA hardware. But what distinguishes the epigenome from the genome is much more complex than any metaphor can convey. Unlike our genome, which remains unchanged throughout our lives, our epigenome is constantly changing. While our DNA markers are duplicated to produce exact copies, our epigenetic markers change according to our environment. They are particularly sensitive to stress, pollution, and diet, as well as exercise and sleep. When we live under stress, such as in poverty or in toxic environments, the strain begins to corrupt our genetic machinery.

We pass those harmful epigenetic markers on from generation to generation, shortening the lives of our offspring and theirs, because our epigenome is passed down to our descendants alongside the DNA in our cells. We know this because of the many epigenetic studies that have focused on how trauma is inherited from major sociohistorical events. Studies of famines such as the Dutch Hunger Winter, in which Nazis prevented food from reaching Dutch citizens, and of internments, like those involving Jews in the Holocaust and prisoners of war during the US Civil War, show that harmful epigenetic modifications can accumulate in people who are socially classified one way or another according to their nationality, political status, ethnicity, and race. These studies indicate that people who suffer discrimination based on these social constructs are predisposed to a host of diseases such as anxiety, diabetes, obesity, PTSD, and schizophrenia. These DNA modifications and their disease predispositions are then passed on to their offspring and their offspring's offspring, for generations to come.

Within epigenetic science, one research area focuses on racial "weathering," or racism's toll on a person's epigenome. Studies have found that adverse exposures like stress, violence, and contamination harmfully reprogram the epigenome with new regulatory patterns that genome scientists call "signatures," and that those signatures can be detected for generations after the initial exposure. For instance, a woman who grows up under slavery may have epigenetic markers that are degraded by the stressors of extreme work, poverty, inadequate diet, and emotional uncertainty. Her daughter, in turn, may inherit epigenetic markers impacted by that history.

Epigenetic studies of racial weathering build on a long tradition of nongenomic epidemiological weathering research that has revealed the ways in which racism and racial biases signal and sign their names onto our cellular inner workings. Inside the body are our organ systems and cells, but conditioning that biological reality is the broader social reality of interactions and experiences that are structured by our belief in race. Decades of epidemiological studies on weathering have revealed that racial discrimination prematurely ages minoritized bodies, regardless of gender, class, and age. A person seen as a racial minority, experiencing discrimination, is less likely to have a long and healthy life.

Given that the body is particularly vulnerable to the environment during pregnancy, many epidemiologists have focused on the disproportionate risks that minoritized pregnant women and their children face. Scientists from an array of health science fields have determined that our most "micro" biology is a figment of our most "macro" social relations. A mass of epidemiological studies has shown that Black women have worse prenatal, birth, and postnatal outcomes than White women due to the racism they experience in their daily lives and the early aging they have suffered up to that point, and Black women are three times as likely as White women to die in childbirth. Research into the poorer health status of embryos and fetuses carried by minoritized women suggests that even the smallest unit of biology, a zygote, is greatly influenced by our social beliefs about race.

Epigenetic studies on racial weathering have since substantiated the broader finding that maternal environments are particularly responsive to the social environment, with pregnant women and newborns of color exhibiting high rates of harmful DNA modifications that turn off genes essential to the healthy functioning of embryos and fetuses. In recent years, epigenetic science has also shown that early life experiences of racial discrimination can permanently damage a person's stress-response system. Children of color who have inherited harmful epigenetic signatures and who face racial discrimination in their daily lives are forced into chronic stress cycles that wear and tear their bodies. People of color who have experienced racial discrimination alongside stressful life events like loss of a parent or abuse in early childhood have exhibited some of the highest levels of epigenetic wear and tear seen in humans, and they have accumulated much higher risks for debilitating diseases than Whites. Black and Latinx people in America in particular have been shown to possess a range of harmful epigenetic markers that predispose them to neurodegenerative and autoimmune disorders. Along with premature aging, Black and Latinx Americans are further weathered by earlier onsets of disease and poorer prognoses than others.

———

NEW PROMISING MODELS OF systems biology—the study of dynamic interactions between the components of our biological systems—also help us to see the destructive relationship of racial classification, discrimination, identity, and genomics. Like epigenetics, models of systems biology reveal how the most external-seeming factors of society, such as racism and bias, impact the most internal-seeming factors of our cells, such as cell signaling and reproduction. These models help focus a new lens on race so that we can reconstruct it in a way that simultaneously dismantles racism and genetic determinism.

One extremely compelling model of race and genomics is biologist Anne Fausto-Sterling's approach to labeling embedded systems of race. Fausto-Sterling shows us that physiological differences that we attribute to race are mediated by the socioeconomic and racial inequality in our social environments. She asks us to see genomic systems as nested in larger physiological systems, which themselves are nested in individual systems, social systems, cultural systems, and more.

Fausto-Sterling gives the example of bone density, which many researchers and healthcare providers characterize as genomically different in members of different races, with Blacks suffering the highest post-fracture mortality rates. In reality, one's bone density is determined by a complicated interplay of genetic and social factors. Fausto-Sterling shows that the genetic variants associated with vitamin D production in our cells (which contrary to popular assumption are distributed gradually and continuously across the globe and not racially) are embedded in specific intracellular regulatory systems (epigenetic and hormone signaling systems), which are embedded in cells (osteocytes), which are embedded in organs (bones), which are embedded in inter-organ regulatory pathways (bone-brain-circulatory-muscle-skin systems). Then there are the routine activities in which these inter-organ regulatory pathways are themselves embedded (walking, resting, exercising). In addition are the individual systems that frame those (living and working conditions) and are activated and located in interpersonal interactions (social relationships of power).

The interpersonal actions, of course, don't take place in a vacuum. They are embedded in and conditioned by cultural practices (racism and bias) that are embedded in social hierarchies (access to healthy food and environments, health literacy, and health resources). Cultural practices arise within the specific geographical context in which they are embedded (i.e., Jamaica during slavery, the United States during Jim Crow). And all of this has both a short-term and long-term history, not the least of which includes an evolutionary history that embeds geography but also geography's relationship to and embeddedness in processes of natural selection. Bone density, disease, and disease outcomes present differently for different races because of racial inequality, not genes. Ignoring these embedded systems of race, we misattribute the social reality of race to genetics.

MY OWN LOOK INTO the sociology and genomics of skin color—one of the most common ways that people characterize race—similarly shows that skin color also appears to us as different in different races because of our tendency to categorize by race and not genes. Skin color isn't the same for all members of a race. Instead, skin color is "clinal"—it forms a geographical gradient across the planet. The distribution of the color that actually exists in humans, as well as the genetic variants associated with that color, in no way corresponds to race despite the racial differences that we believe we see.

Haplotypic analysis of pigmentation differences reveals that skin color is so continuously distributed across the world that genetics cannot even begin to explain its diversity. While the trait may have once traced an evolutionary pattern in which those whose ancestors lived for many generations closest to the Earth's poles displayed the least amount of pigmentation and those whose ancestors lived for many generations closest to the equator displayed the most pigmentation, today the pigmentation of Arctic groups like the lyg'oravetl'a, or Chukchi, is on par with equatorial groups like the Yanomami. How close your ancestors once lived to the equator is not the only determiner of your skin color; many more factors are at play.

Mapping the genes associated with the expression of human pigmentation further problematizes our most common assumptions about skin color and race. Two genes are heavily involved in human skin pigmentation: the melanocortin receptor gene called *MC1R* and the solute carrier gene *SLC24A5*. *MC1R* is responsible for producing two types of melanin that combine to determine the color of a person's skin and hair, as well as their photosensitivity. *SLC24A5*, which also contributes to our color and photosensitivity, regulates just how much of that melanin is produced at a given time in a person's cells.

MC1R is what researchers call a "highly conserved" gene. It is found in all kinds of organisms, from fish to mice to primates. The same goes for *SLC24A5*, which was first discovered and studied in fish. These genes are a perfect example of how traits we attribute racial meaning to exist to help bodies function across many species, for the basic health of all.

There are differences in the frequencies of genetic variants that regulate pigmentation, but none of these variants are the property of one human population or another. Furthermore, how a person looks does not always correspond with their underlying genotype (the specific nucleotides that regulate melanin production). In the United

States alone, one quarter of the nation's population has a red-hair version of the *MC1R* gene, yet only 2 to 6 percent of Americans report having red hair. Meanwhile, dysfunctional variations of *SLC24A5* that lead to albinism (lack of pigmentation) have been found in groups living all over the world though albinism only affects 1 in 17,000 people worldwide.

Looking at another trait associated with race—hair texture—we can similarly see that genes like the trichohyalin gene *TCHH*, which structures the skin and hair in and around hair follicles, and the ecto-dysplasin gene *EDA*, which assists us in producing skin, hair, sweat glands, and teeth, are also conserved across animal species and exist continuously across the globe. *TCHH* is found in all mammals living around the planet; there are even homologous genes in birds and reptiles that help them develop their feathers and scaly skin. As with skin color, much of what we know about hair texture comes from research into dental and epidermal problems in fish, revealing that vertebrates share these important genes no matter how similar or different they appear to us and how far and wide we search.

We see and attribute differences in skin color and hair texture to race because the racialism in our society has convinced us there are racial differences. Similarly, we attribute the differences we see in race to genomics, and not to the social context of racialism and racism, because genetic determinism has convinced us there are continental races. In reality, as Fausto-Sterling's model has it, genetic variants for skin color and hair texture are embedded in and modified by a person's environment, including their nutrition, exercise, and exposure to the sun. And those biological processes are themselves embedded in cultural practices and living and working conditions that structure how we live.

No racial conclusion can be drawn from genomic mapping of so-called racial differences. Genomic analysis shows just the opposite: genomic structure and function are the property of all. Therefore it is important to understand the difference between genomics and race. Genomic science studies genetic ancestry, tracing human migrations and the diseases that have evolved as humans have moved within and between continents many times over. Genomic science tells us about ancestry, not race. As easy as it is to think that biological differences we observe are racial, our DNA tells us that genetic variation is continuous. There is no such thing as genomic race.

It's a lot to wrap your mind around; however, it is much more accurate and therefore representative of the reality of race and genomics. To Fausto-Sterling's systems biology model I would add political history, sociological history, and other structural factors—the full context of our lives and therefore our complete reality.

By analyzing all these aspects of our lives, we can begin to capitalize on the upside of our epigenomics and biological systems. Our DNA is not our destiny. Changes to social policy that create healthy environments for all humans—removing lead from gas, chemicals from food, and racism and bias from our social environments—can rewrite the bad and proliferate the good. Guided by the basic evolutionary tenet that our environment influences our genes, we can improve our odds. More equitable social policies guided by sociologically informed genomic research into race can improve the health of our DNA and our society.

THESE INNOVATIVE METHODS FOR understanding race and biology prove that we can bring race into our analyses to take it apart and expose the complex processes that are at work. This is a far cry from the inaccurate ways of using race to untangle racism in science such as using race as a proxy for genetics, calling genetic populations by racial labels, pooling samples by race, or distributing DNA data by race.

In the early 2000s, when major global DNA collections were first being amassed, and when genomic researchers first engaged in strategic essentialism as a tactic to get more people of color involved in research, structuring genomic databases by race seemed like the right thing to do. Mobilizing researchers to foster racial fraternity by encouraging the participation of people of color who felt reluctant made sense to project leaders. Strategically reinforcing the biological kinship of race appeared the best starting point for genome mappers to diversify genomic science, as Latinx genomics specialist Esteban Burchard once put it. But today, the fortification of racialized DNA collections has only led to a racial apparatus that cannot move beyond that starting point.

Now more than ever we need interdisciplinary research that can show how our systems of race affect our systems of biology. We need projects and studies that involve genome scientists, health scientists, social scientists, racial justice advocates and activists, and members of communities that experience racism to partner, bringing their diverse angles and methods to the table. It must be a balanced effort where all sides steer research equitably. When genomic research overwhelms the social and behavioral research and people's lived experiences, we get devastatingly deterministic conclusions that reinforce biological notions of race. Without a balanced *trans*disciplinary effort that is inclusive of the public, even the most well-intentioned researchers will vastly mishandle race.

We also need to support the design and deployment of algorithms that counter the racial structuring of research. When genomic racialism infiltrates more areas of research, especially research about behavioral traits like intelligence and criminality, we generate more virulent forms of genomic racism. Tragically, the social and behavioral genomic research in some of our best attempts at transdisciplinary science is still working with highly racialized data—the very databases that project leaders like Burchard believed would be a mere starting point. For example, the UK Biobank, which labels samples as "White," "Asian," "Black," or "Mixed," and the 23andMe collection, which is labeled by "major ethnicity"—what 23andMe refers to as "populations that existed before transcontinental travel and migration were common (at least 500 years ago)"—are still the primary sources for social and behavioral research.

We also need to prioritize understanding and assisting study subjects with the issues that cause racial inequality in their lives. Despite the participation of social scientists with sophisticated understandings of racial injustice in genomic research, we continue to see minority inclusion in research—that is, sampling the DNA of groups of color that have traditionally been underserved by genetic science—posed as the be-all and end-all of racially equitable science. Even when minority scientists who are deeply and personally concerned about racial inequality lead the charge to include more minority study subjects in DNA collections, they elide sociological factors of racism and bias. The end result is a growing sociogenomic literature based on gene hunts for specific behaviors, with no light shed on the role of race in participants' lives.

We need inclusion for good, not inclusion that breeds more racism. Researchers continue to tell reporters that they are ashamed of the Eurocentrism of past and present genetic and genomic sciences, and they continue to reassure the public that they are using racially diverse datasets. Yet when headlines report that genome scientists have found variants for aggression or intelligence or entrepreneurialism in one race or another, it is nearly impossible for people to renounce racialism or genetic determinism and reject the notion that there is something genetically exceptional and consonant about the genomes of specific racial groups.

In my work with the National Academies of Science, Engineering and Medicine, as well as the National Human Genome Research Institute and the NIH, I have concluded that there is only one way forward: to eliminate racial classification from genomic research reporting unless the study is explicitly about the biological effects of racism and bias.

The only reason to use racial classifications is to study issues pertaining to race, such as how experiencing racial discrimination impacts a person's blood pressure or how suffering implicit bias corresponds with premature aging. There must be a clear rationale for seeking answers in biology and genomics, plus proof of a relationship between genomic processes and social processes of race.

A more rigorous and meaningful way for other researchers to include racial minorities in genomic research would be to recruit people of different backgrounds using the labels that they prefer in recruitment and enrollment, and then to drop those labels in the process of logging samples into a database. There is no reason to reinscribe racial classifications into DNA collections. And there is definitely no reason to store and issue DNA data by OMB or continental race.

Another useful way to diversify research would be to recruit more people from underserved ethnic groups *within* minoritized races to show the diversity of their genetics, social environments, and health and illness experiences. Because Africa has been racialized as "Black," and because scientists have thereby ignored the vast majority of its ethnic groups, researchers continue to make a few groups stand in for thousands of others. It is scientifically false and socially harmful to posit specific groups as generalizable to all Black people worldwide.

We don't need just any kind of inclusion and we certainly don't need just any kind of research. We need research that holds race's mutability—its constructed social reality—at its core. Instead of affixing racial labels on analyses that in reality have nothing to do with race and racism—as genetic research has for so long—let's use racial labels only when we are truly studying race: namely, racial discrimination, racial inequality, and the ways in which institutionalized racism, prejudice, and violence get under our skin, whatever color it is. We must leverage what we experience socially and politically to understand the real connection between race and genetics.

I SHARE THESE RECOMMENDATIONS because, though you may never conduct your own research into race, it is important to be able to scrutinize the claims of researchers who do. Every study that invokes race is constructing it. We must ask ourselves how we can support research that constructs race for the better. To this end, I have developed three litmus tests.

One test for whether a model that researchers are working with is responsibly constructing race is to consider whether it includes a measure for racial discrimination. If the study invokes race, does it have an explicit method of ascertaining racism and/or racialism? Do its racial categories represent these metrics of inequality? For every invocation of racial difference, there must be a clear marker of social difference (e.g., toxic work or living conditions, microaggressions or stress) that is explained by the lived realities of research subjects.

A second test for a responsible construction of race is to determine whether the model accounts for the feedback loops created by racism and racialism. Here I turn to Troy Duster's sage words about conducting a "systematic investigation . . . into the role of the interaction of 'race' . . . however flawed . . . with feedback loops into the biological functioning of the human body." Duster maintains that the starting point of race will always be some event of racial mistreatment, in the clinic or in the community. Have subjects been overprescribed medication or gone undiagnosed because of their perceived race? Have they been unable to sleep due to a toxic job or home? From there, the researcher's job is to trace the echoes of this discrimination or inequality in concrete biological processes, from the outermost rings of the stress-response to the innermost rings of epigenetic health. Studies not only must be dynamic enough to capture these reverberations but also must follow the trail from the original event inward, documenting the snowball effect of the initial social harm. The analysis must always move in that direction from, as Duster calls it, "race used as a stratifying practice" to the inner workings of our minds and bodies.

A third test is to appraise whether a study has clear and evident policy implications. Here I draw from Alondra Nelson's concept of "social health" that members of the Black Panther Party conceived in their revolutionary health science. As Nelson explains, social health was "scaled from the individual, corporeal body to the body politic in such a way that therapeutic matters were inextricably articulated to social justice ones." Every aspect of the Panthers' health science had to document, analyze, characterize, and explain these varying aspects of health and provide alternative politics so that social justice could be achieved. I want to adapt this understanding to how we look at today's science that invokes race. As evident in epigenetic weathering studies and studies that illuminate the feedback loops of genomic health and society, there will always be a clear political implication from the insights gleaned. A responsible study will always be up front about those implications, ensuring that they can impact the very populations under study.

Antiracism in genomics proper is not realistic. But antiracism in a transdisciplinary science that constructs race with and for the people is. For racialism to truly be antiracist and not unwittingly deterministic, studies must break down how race is made real and illuminate the alternative sociopolitical reality for us to pursue.

CHAPTER 8

The Reality of Race

M Y EXPERIENCES AND RESEARCH HAVE taught me a great deal about what's real about race, the unyielding social reality that has gripped humanity for so long. Race started as an invention—a technology of power conceived in the Enlightenment era—and it has snowballed into a structuring ideology—a belief system that implicates every institution of our lives. Race has seeded, rooted, and germinated in our centuries of seeing, thinking, knowing, and interacting to the point where it stands as a focal point for how we make meaning of the world within us and around us, how we construct our social reality, and how we coexist.

Race is also a legacy of paradigms that have failed us. Enlightenment Race established our centuries-long convention of grouping people by continental ancestry and ranking them from better to worse on a collection of mental and physiological attributes. Modern Race colored this continental ranking system with eugenics, inspiring immigration bans, sterilization policies, and mass genocide. UNESCO Race countered the narrative of White supremacy and White Nationalism with an argument for mutual fitness and peaceful coexistence, but it failed to dismantle the false narrative of continental genetic races. And though Genomic Race has carried forth UNESCO Race's message of equality of races, it too has inadvertently upheld the long-standing belief that races are different due to genetics. Today, we desperately need a new paradigm of race as well as a new language for talking about race, which I have been trying to develop as I speak with our youth. And as I raise my own children, I spend a great deal of time discussing race with them. I give them the education that my friend Kaiya and I never had.

I try to explain how we all invest in beliefs and make them real in words that make sense to developing minds. We value some things over others, mostly those things that other people have told us are worth valuing. We construct categories just the way we would a house of blocks. In fact, we make entire worlds around these made-up categories, building them into every nook and cranny of our social worlds until no one remembers what was there before.

I tell my kids that people will see them as light-skinned and mixed, and that they will be compared with others who are dark-skinned and judged a different race because we have been taught to see race as tied to skin color. Some people rank. Some just distinguish. Others talk about race as a spectrum of qualities. Nevertheless, the fact is that people agree on the existence of difference and see it all around them. That belief is what makes race real.

Other issues about which I talk to my kids include identity: there are moments when we identify with a particular idea of race, when we see ourselves as something or other, when we "identify *as*."* I have

* In *The Ethics of Identity*, philosopher of race Kwame Anthony Appiah discusses identity as a process of identifying and being identified in terms of the many taxonomies that structure our lives.

identified on various forms and in different circumstances as Pacific Islander, as Asian, as a person of color, as mixed race, as Brown. We may imagine ourselves to be connected to a group or groups for cultural reasons, or moral or intellectual ones. We may feel connected biologically, genetically, hereditarily. We may identify ourselves strategically for political purposes or, by contrast, for no conscious reason at all.

Another issue is assuming the race of others: there are moments when we are seeing people in terms of a particular idea of race, when we "see others *as*." We categorize others and ascribe them identities for all the reasons listed above, yet too often with the effect of harming them despite our personal intentions. There are even moments in which we ourselves are being categorized, or ascribed a race, when others are "identifying me *as*." These moments are often as ordinary as filling out a form, as unremarkable as standing in a line, as automatic as just barely being noticed.

I teach my kids to be critical so that they can recognize that seeing does not have to be believing—we don't have to be locked into other people's value systems concerning race. Contrary to what grownups and peers in the world out there will say, race is *not* genetics. There are no genes that belong to one race and no other races. There are no racial divisions in our genomes. There are no distinct races divided by continent.

Likewise, there are no biological pathways (cardiovascular, renal, psychiatric, etc.) that function uniquely for one race or another. There is no scientific merit to the biological divisions (skin color, hair texture, eye and nose shape, etc.) that we invoke when we categorize by race. There is no such thing as the superiority and inferiority of different races.

Instead, I teach my children to see what's real about race—namely, its materiality in our social ties and experiences. Race manifests in the array of familial bonds, friendships, school cliques, and work circles, and all the opportunities and lack of opportunity those social connections afford. Race is also made real through the litany of micro- and macroaggressions, the implicit and explicit biases, the prejudice and structural racism that privilege those categorized as White and punish those categorized as "of color." Nothing more clearly substantiates race than the vast disparities in outcomes of pregnancy, birth, health and disease, and life and death between Whites and people of color. Yet despite existing all around us, not everyone is trained to see these inequities.

I also teach my children to see that what's real about race are the fictions: our faulty beliefs about racial differences. These beliefs too inform whom we love, how we see ourselves, and what kinds of dreams we can access.

Finally, I encourage them to understand the malleability of their ideas and thoughts so that they can be aware of the problems with seeing race. Regardless of how mundane or unconscious these moments of noticing race may seem, they are a part of a powerful cognitive feedback loop. The brain harnesses its power of attention. It retrieves past memories. It brings up old emotions and imprints new ones. And in most situations, when we notice race, no matter how routine the instance is, the feedback loop kicks up stress. This is the very real cycle of perception that, no matter how brief, engraves race in our minds and emotions. This cycle makes race real in our psychology as much as externally, ensuring race an ongoing meaning in our lives.

By showing my kids how to be aware of race's emotional impact, and by teaching them that race is being made in our minds and interactions when we least expect it, I am empowering them to do what Kaiya and I tried to do: acknowledge racialization and make it explicit. Having that awareness in mind, they can, I hope, think critically about race. They can perceive race and navigate a racist world in novel, empathetic, and equitable ways.

I ALSO SPEND A lot of time teaching my older "kids"—my undergraduate students—to see these things and to commit to *de*-constructing race. News cycles spend a lot of air time on explosive racist acts, usually motivated by White supremacy, and we talk about those events in my classes too. However, as devastating as massacres and police killings are, these racist events aren't the only reason that race remains central to our lives. It is the way that race is woven into our daily experiences that makes it a reality.

I tell my students that protesting, participating in racial advocacy struggles, and joining a movement are ways of enacting resistance to racial injustice. Yet change can also take root and flourish through our everyday thoughts and actions. After all, there is another two-ness about race worth paying attention to: race is both ideological and material. It is a matter of beliefs, and yet it is built into the fabric of our social environment.

We can't just stop talking about race and stop seeing it, hoping that racism will abate. We must instead talk about it more, draw others' attention to it, and fight against racism.

With novel scientific platforms like systems biology and traditional means like storytelling, we can decouple race from genetics and understand how racism impacts our bodies and societies—the true meaning of antiracism. As historian Ibram X. Kendi argues, the opposite of racism isn't *non*racism, but rather active *anti*racism. Silence and inaction make us complicit. And by being complicit, we aid racism. In other words, we are being racist. We are supporting racist ideology and racist practice, and we are abetting a system in which structural racism reigns supreme. I therefore ask my students to consider how they might use their own platforms, now and going forward as they pursue their dreams, to give voice to the social reality of race.

I rose from my own experience as a racially marginalized youth to become a scholar of race. Strikingly, my friend Kaiya did too. She went on to become a leader in environmental racial justice in America, whose work is impacting lives and healing the racism that threatens our species. Together we stand with antiracists who have dedicated their life's work to elevating our collective awareness of race so we can change our circumstances at the level of our material reality.

As sociologist Ruha Benjamin urges, "Remember to imagine and craft the worlds you cannot live without, just as you dismantle the ones you cannot live within." Her words remind us that the deconstruction and reconstruction of race is a world-making material undertaking with material consequences in our everyday realities. Our biological lives literally depend on the social reality of it. We need everyone on board to make a systems-level revolution if we are to radically end racism.

IF RACE IS SO ruinous, what can we do? Is living with race inevitable? Is it a permanent reality? And whether we are stuck with it or not, can it be improved?

It is critical to recognize that race means many things to many people (and many different things to individual people at any given moment). Race has been a source of solidarity even as it has promoted tyranny. People of color living under racial domination have created illustrious works of philosophy, sociology, psychology, anthropology, and biology. People living in systems of racial oppression have transformed our understandings of liberty, equality, fraternity, humanity, what makes humans human, and how humans know themselves, relate to each other, and care for and love one another. Art, music, dance, photography, film, all manifested and perfected by the racially oppressed: none of these exist absent of, or bracketed from, our reality of race.

In the United States, a multicultural, multiethnic, and multinational country that is set to be majority non-White by 2044, polls show that the majority of people who self-identify as other than White say race is extremely or very important to them, while almost half of all people who self-identify as White say that it is not at all. Yet the same Whites who say that race is not important are fearful about race relations. And people of color are fearful as well; many of them agree that we must erase racism, or "eracism," but disagree with the idea of erasing race from the national dialogue.

The United States is not alone. Countries all around the world, even those that have never been governed by colonial rule or had a White majority, are experiencing civil unrest around the struggle for equality between majority and minority groups. To foster equality in all these places, we need a better understanding of what's real about race. As much as we wish that we could get rid of racial categories, they are baked into our society. So instead we must imbue race with new meaning as activists and intellectuals have done for so long. We must replace our false narratives about race with a deeper understanding of the social reality of race by turning to three important sources of knowledge.

The first source comprises racially oppressed people who by virtue of their race routinely experience racism. We need to listen to their individual experiences, their wisdom, their hopes, dreams, desires. We need to spawn strategy from their firsthand knowledge. We need to elevate their voices in spite of the dominant voices that would have them remain silent.

The second source comprises the social sciences and humanities—politics, law, sociology, psychology, anthropology, philosophy, and the many fields of art that analyze and explain racial inequality. We must expose how laws that produce structural racism, like school segregation and barriers to citizenship, bring about inequality. We must also expose how less explicit policies and customs, like classifying by race in education and criminal justice, do too. Finally, we must unearth the many racial biases in our education systems and healthcare facilities, and begin to rout them in administration, teaching, and patient care.

The third source comprises life sciences like genomic science, evolutionary biology, epidemiology, and environmental studies, fields that remain our most authoritative and final word on how our environments impact our DNA. Though I have spent much of this book warning of the disaster caused by allowing genetic science to rule racial discourse, those of us working in biomedicine and health sciences must use our power to challenge the idea that race is just genetics. We must correct any false narratives we see that promote the idea that races are genetically distinct, and that racial inequality is inevitably emblazoned in our DNA.

But lest we reinforce the notion that only genomic science can define race, we need more sociopolitically focused research like epigenetic, systems biology, and sociologically oriented genomic research. We need studies that look at the relationship between our bodies and our beliefs. How do our policies and politics structure systems of opportunity in everyday life? How does a lack of resources and exposures get under our skin and into our cells and embed in the very DNA-based control mechanisms that tell our bodies to wither or thrive?

Neuroscience and genetic epidemiology have similarly taught us that racism sets into effect a cascade of crises in our minds and bodies. Chronic racism in the form of microaggressions and internalized threats cycles damaging hormones from the brain to the major organs. Studies of genetics and skin color have found that people with darker skin are at higher risk for high blood pressure even when they are younger and healthier than their lighter-skinned counterparts due to an inordinate share of racial stress. In other words, the toll of discrimination can precipitate disease in otherwise healthy individuals just because of their perceived race.

In sum, a radical way of approaching race is needed now more than ever, and this requires a radical look at reality. Privileging accounts of race and studies of racism that see the vast interconnected networks of our various biosocial, gene-environment systems will allow us to move beyond the limited contemporary approaches that are particularly vulnerable to racist distortion and systematization.

Race, the idea and the material thing that it is, is hitting us on all these levels of reality. It is too easy for the language of "social construct" to become nonracist, not antiracist. And then what are we left with but complicity, otherwise known as racism. We need explicit language that can wake us up to the real and life-threatening thing that is race. This is why I ask that we stop calling race a social construct and start calling it a social reality.

When I'm asked what's real about race, this is what I say: Race is a complicated combination of social, structural, and material factors, and must be viewed as such. If we mistakenly view race as a genetic category and ignore the many social factors that construct our differences, we perpetuate an inaccurate view of what's real about race. Race isn't in our DNA. Race doesn't determine our intelligence or our behavior. But that doesn't mean it isn't real. Race often holds personal meanings for us, which shouldn't be discounted. Race, and racism, are a part of our history. And, more than likely, they're part of our future. Identity categories are always evolving, but they're unlikely to disappear anytime soon. We'll probably always encounter mistaken ideas about identity and biology. But when we misunderstand what race is and isn't, as even well-intentioned genomic scientists, educators, and policymakers often do, we end up rationalizing injustice through false, unscientific distinctions.

We must continue to advocate for the truths that historians, social scientists, genomic scientists, and researchers have illuminated: that racial difference on a biological level is a myth, but that racism and its structural impacts shape our health, opportunities, and lives in major ways. If we're invested in creating a world that's livable for everyone, we need to advocate for these truths in every circumstance, whether that's in education policy, drug research, or in our own communities. Only then can we create a more equitable reality.

ACKNOWLEDGMENTS

SO MANY INTERVIEWS, CONVERSATIONS, DISCUSSIONS, and loving dialogues moved me to write this book, and I am grateful to all who inspired me. Above all, I give thanks to my soul sister, Ruha Benjamin, who recommended that I write this book, and my nearest and dearest in my home community of Princeton, Emily Merchant, Alondra Nelson, and Janet Vertesi.

Thanks are due to too many to name in the genomics and sociogenomics communities, but I give a special shout out to Matt Hudson, Aaron Panofsky, and Gene Robinson, as well as my key interlocutors, Jason Boardman, Vence Bonham, Aravinda Chakravarti, Emmanuelle Charpentier, George Church, Francis Collins, Dalton Conley, Philipp Koellinger, Sandra Soo-Jin Lee, Jonathan Marks, Melinda Mills, Joanna Mountain, and Craig Venter.

My deepest gratitude goes to my race and genetics research and writing group, especially Catherine Lee, Ann Morning, and Wendy Roth, and all my race and genetics working group fellows at Duke, Harvard, and the University of California, with a special thanks to

Jennifer Eberhardt, Henry Louis Gates Jr., Joseph Graves, Evelynn Hammonds, Nina Jablonski, Terrence Keel, Rick Kittles, Barbara Koenig, Osagie Obasogie, Michael Omi, Neil Risch, and Howard Winant. Troy Duster deserves a special mention here for helping me think through the thorniest social implications of race and genetics. His love and mentorship shine through all my writing.

I also want to thank my colleagues at Rutgers, especially my lead researcher, Marilyn Baffoe-Bonnie (go Dr. Marilyn!), and my former colleagues at UCSF, Janet Shim and Howard Pinderhughes, for helping me work through the foundations of this book.

With this book I have had the greatest pleasure to work with some of the most remarkable hearts and minds in publishing, and I am grateful to the whole team at Norton. Express thanks go to Alane Mason and Michael Moss for conceiving the idea for this book, as well as Tom Mayer for taking it from concept to manuscript. Special appreciation goes to Caroline Adams for providing the keenest editorial vision and leadership, and to Meredith Dowling and Kyle Radler for making magic with marketing and publicity.

My team of agents at Aevitas Creative Management, Best Make Do, Outspoken Agency, and Posco Publicity has buoyed me through the writing and beyond. I am so grateful for Will Lippincott, who is not only my biggest rep but also my guide and inspiration. I am deeply appreciative of Kristin Steele for breathing creative life into my virtual being. I thank Megan Posco for her phenomenal brand wisdom and keen eye toward message. I also thank everybody at Outspoken, especially Tara Berthier, Tori Marra, and Catie Bradley Shea. A big shout goes to Ashton Marra for her word wizardry. I am a better scholar and intellectual thanks to their support and efforts.

In writing this book, I benefited from the generosity of many people in my home community. The "village" it took to produce this book consisted of Princeton and Institute for Advanced Study families and educators too numerous to name, but I want to give special recognition to Nelly Alvarado, Lydia McDaniel, Melissa O'Donnell, Danielle Otis, Luis Ramirez, and Christine Trautman.

Finally, I want to say a huge thank you to my friends and family far and wide, especially those walking through life with me here in Princeton, and those making our visits back to California, Jakarta, Massachusetts, New York, and Surabaya memorable. The Blisses, Caryabudis, and Woodburys fill me up in every way. I wouldn't and couldn't exist without them. Most of all, Nick Woodbury and our littles to whom I have dedicated this book. You are the best reality I could ever ask for!

NOTES

INTRODUCTION

8   **Their efforts had not:** Bliss, Catherine. *Race Decoded: The Genomic Fight for Social Justice.* Stanford University Press, 2012.

9   **I found that much of the genetics:** Robinson, G.E., C.M. Grozinger, and C.W. Whitfield, 2005. "Sociogenomics: Social Life in Molecular Terms." *Nature Reviews Genetics* 6 (4): 257–270.

9   **US population projections:** Frey, William H. "New Projections Point to a Majority Minority Nation in 2044." Brookings, Dec. 14, 2018. www.brookings.edu/articles/new-projections-point-to-a-majority-minority-nation-in-2044/.

10   **Suddenly, genetic notions:** Bliss, Catherine. *Social by Nature: The Promise and Peril of Sociogenomics.* Stanford University Press, 2018.

11   **Human intelligence is an:** Bliss, Rina. *Rethinking Intelligence: A Radical New Understanding of Our Human Potential.* HarperCollins, 2023.

CHAPTER 1: A BRIEF HISTORY OF RACE

17   **Before there was race:** Woolf, Greg. *The Life and Death of Ancient Cities: A Natural History.* Oxford University Press, 2020; Watson, James. "The Origin of Metic Status at Athens." *The Cambridge Classical Journal* 56 (2010): 259–278; Twitchett, Denis, and Michael Loewe. *The Cambridge History of China.* Cambridge University Press, 1986; Cornelius, Sakkie. "Ancient Egypt and the Other." *Scriptura* 104, no. 1 (2010): 322–340.

20   **In 1665, François:** Bernier, François, and Irving Brock. *Travels in the Mogul Empire.* W. Pickering, 1826.

20   **Based on his assessments:** Bernier, François. "A New Division of the Earth." *Journal des Sçavans,* Apr. 24, 1684, pp. 148–155.

21   **After completing a two-week doctorate:** Linné, Carl von. *Systema Naturae, sive Regna Tria Naturae Systematice Proposita per Classes, Ordines, Genera & Species.* Haak, 1735.

22   **Subsequent naturalists of:** Georges-Louis Leclerc, Comte de Buffon. "Of the Varieties in the Human Species." In *Natural History, General and Particular,* translated by William Smellie, vol. 3, pp. 449–510. W. Strahan and T. Cadell, 1781; Blumenbach, Johann Friedrich. *De generis humani varietate nativa.* University of Göttingen, 1775; Kant, Immanuel. *The Cambridge Edition of the Works of Immanuel Kant.* Edited by Paul Guyer and Allen W. Wood. Cambridge University Press, 1992.

23   **These scholars maintained that:** Blumenbach. *De generis humani varietate nativa*; Cuvier, George. "An Instructive Note on the Researches to Be Carried out Relative to the Anatomical Differences Between the Diverse Races of Man." 1800.

24   **In his groundbreaking work:** Darwin, Charles. *On the Origin of Species by Means of Natural Selection, or the Preservation of Favoured Races in the Struggle for Life.* John Murray, 1859.

24   **Although he deeply disfavored:** Darwin, Charles. *The Descent of Man, and Selection in Relation to Sex.* John Murray, 1871.

25   **Darwin inspired his cousin:** Galton, Francis. *Hereditary Genius: An Inquiry into Its Laws and Consequences.* Macmillan, 1869; Galton, Francis. "Eugenics: Its Definition, Scope and Aims." *American Journal of Sociology* 10, no. 1 (1904): 1–25.

26   **A cadre of scholars:** Agassiz, Louis. "The Diversity of Origin of the Human Races." *Christian Examiner* 49 (1850): 110–138; Gliddon, George R., J.C. Nott, Louis Agassiz, and W. Usher. *Types of Mankind: Or, Ethnological Researches Based upon the Ancient Monuments, Paintings, Sculptures, and Crania of Races.* Lippincott, Grambo & Co., 1854.

26   **The first census, taken:** United States Bureau of the Census. *Heads of Families at the First Census of the United States Taken in the Year 1790.* Government Printing Office, 1907–1908.

27   **Internationally acclaimed works on:** Down, J. Langdon. "Observations on an Ethnic Classification of Idiots." *Clinical Lectures and Reports,* London Hospital 3 (1866): 259–262; Boas, Franz. *The Mind of Primitive Man.* Rev. ed. Macmillan Company, 1938.

29   **In 1912, the world's:** "Problems in Eugenics Volume II: Report of Proceedings of the First International Eugenics Congress." The Eugenics Education Society, 1913.

30   **For the next meeting:** International Congress of Eugenics. 2nd ed. (1921);
      Charles Benedict Davenport. "Scientific Papers of the Second International
      Congress of Eugenics." Williams & Wilkins Co, 1923.

30   **For example, when Bhagat:** United States v. Bhagat Singh Thind, 261 U.S.
      204 (1923).

31   **Both it and Germany soon instituted:** Hitler, Adolf. *Mein Kampf.* Trans-
      lated by Ralph Manheim. Houghton Mifflin, 1999.

32   **The UN also established:** United Nations Educational, Scientific and Cul-
      tural Organization. "Constitution of the United Nations Educational, Sci-
      entific and Cultural Organization." Nov. 16, 1945. https://www.unesco.org/
      en/legal-affairs/constitution.

32   **Leading scientists from around:** "Statement on Race." UNESCO, 1950;
      "Statement on the Nature of Race and Race Differences." UNESCO, 1951.

35   **In its final edict:** "Race and Ethnic Standards for Federal Statistics and
      Administrative Reporting (Statistical Policy Directive No. 15)." Office of
      Management and Budget, 1977.

CHAPTER 2: THE GENOMICS OF RACE

39   **The Surgeon General and HHS:** United States Public Health Service.
      Office of the Surgeon General. *Healthy People: The Surgeon General's Report
      on Health Promotion and Disease Prevention.* US Dept. of Health, Education,
      and Welfare, Public Health Service, Office of the Assistant Secretary for
      Health, 1979. DHEW Publication No. (PHS) 79–55071; US Department
      of Health and Human Services. "Report of the Secretary's Task Force on
      Black and Minority Health." Washington, D.C., Aug. 1985; US Depart-
      ment of Health and Human Services. "Healthy People 2000: National
      Health Promotion and Disease Prevention Objectives." Washington, D.C.:
      US Government Printing Office, 1990.

39   **When the NIH mandated:** "National Institutes of Health Revitalization
      Act of 1993." Public Law 103–43, US Statutes at Large 107 (1993): 122–159.

40   **In 1997, the FDA:** "Investigational New Drug Applications and New Drug
      Applications" (the Demographic Rule), 63 FR 6854 (Feb. 11, 1998) (codi-
      fied at 21 CFR 312.33(a)(2) and 21 CFR 314.50(d)(5)).

41   **These leaders appeared:** Venter, J. Craig, quoted in Nicholas Wade, "Do
      Races Differ? Not Really, DNA Shows." *The New York Times*, Aug. 22,
      2000.   https://archive.nytimes.com/www.nytimes.com/library/national/
      science/082200sci-genetics-race.html.

41   **At a White House:** "Remarks by the President, Prime Minister Tony Blair of England (via satellite), Dr. Francis Collins, Director of the National Human Genome Research Institute, and Dr. Craig Venter, President and Chief Scientific Officer, Celera Genomics Corporation, on the Completion of the First Survey of the Entire Human Genome Project." The White House, June 26, 2000. https://clintonwhitehouse3.archives.gov/WH/EOP/OSTP/html/00628_2.html.

41   **Yet within months, at:** Collins, Francis S., and Monique K. Mansoura. "The Human Genome Project: Revealing the Shared Inheritance of All Humankind." *Cancer* 91, no. S1 (2001): 221–225.

44   **Project leaders compelled:** The International HapMap Consortium. "Integrating Ethics and Science in the International HapMap Project." *Nature Reviews Genetics* 5 (2004): 467–475.

CHAPTER 3: SEEING AND THINKING RACE

51   **In the mid-1990s, sociologists:** Omi, Michael, and Howard Winant. *Racial Formation in the United States.* 3rd ed. Routledge, 2015.

53   **Similarly, Black, Indigenous, and:** Gilroy, Paul. "The Black Atlantic as a Counterculture of Modernity." In *Theorizing Diaspora.* Edited by Jana Evans Braziel and Anita Mannur. Blackwell, 2003 (originally published in 1995), pp. 49–80. Gilroy. "'After the Love Has Gone': Bio-politics and Etho-poetics in the Black Public Sphere." *Third Text* 8, no. 25 (1994): 25–48.

54   **Experts now understood:** Hall, Stuart. "Race: The Floating Signifier." Transcript. Media Education Foundation, 1997.

54   **Hall's work dovetailed:** Spivak, Gayatri Chakravorty. "Interview with Gayatri Chakravorty Spivak: New Nation Writers Conference in Calgary." Elizabeth Grosz. In *The Post-Colonial Critic: Interviews, Strategies, Dialogues,* edited by Sarah Harasym, 59–66. Routledge, 1990.

56   **more likely to be disciplined:** New York Civil Liberties Union. "A Look at School Discipline." Accessed June 26, 2024. https://www.nyclu.org/report/look-school-discipline.

56   **less likely to be treated:** American Psychiatric Association. "Mental Health Facts for Diverse Populations." Accessed June 26, 2024. https://www.psychiatry.org/getmedia/bac9c998-5b2d-4ffa-ace9-d35844b8475a/Mental-Health-Facts-for-Diverse-Populations.pdf.

60   **Greenwald, and:** Greenwald, A.G., and M.R. Banaji. "Implicit Social

Cognition: Attitudes, Self-Esteem, and Stereotypes." *Psychological Review* 102, no. 1 (1995): 4–27; Greenwald, A.G., D.E. McGhee, and J.L.K. Schwartz. "Measuring Individual Differences in Implicit Cognition: The Implicit Association Test." *Journal of Personality and Social Psychology* 74, no. 6 (1998): 1464–1480; Nosek, B.A., M.R. Banaji, and A.G. Greenwald. "Harvesting Implicit Group Attitudes and Beliefs from a Demonstration Web Site." *Group Dynamics: Theory, Research, and Practice* 6, no. 1 (2002): 101–115.

60 **Every seven or eight:** Nosek, B.A., A.G. Greenwald, and M.R. Banaji. "The Implicit Association Test at Age 7: A Methodological and Conceptual Review." In *Social Psychology and the Unconscious: The Automaticity of Higher Mental Processes*, edited by J.A. Bargh, 265–292. Psychology Press, 2007; Greenwald, A.G., M.R. Banaji, and B.A. Nosek. "Statistically Small Effects of the Implicit Association Test Can Have Societally Large Effects. *Journal of Personality and Social Psychology* 108, no. 4 (2015): 553–561; Kurdi, B., et al. "Relationship Between the Implicit Association Test and Intergroup Behavior: A Meta-Analysis." *American Psychologist* 74, no. 5 (2019): 569–586.

62 **Brain scans and:** Phelps, E.A., et al. "Performance on Indirect Measures of Race Evaluation Predicts Amygdala Activation." *Journal of Cognitive Neuroscience* 12, no. 5 (2000): 729–738; Hart, A.J., et al. "Differential Response in the Human Amygdala to Racial Outgroup vs. Ingroup Face Stimuli." *Neuroreport* 11, no. 11 (2000): 2351–2355; W.A. Cunningham et al. "Separable Neural Components in the Processing of Black and White Faces." *Psychological Science* 15, no. 12 (2004): 806–813; Lieberman, M.D., A. Hariri, J.M. Jarcho, N.I. Eisenberger, and S.Y. Bookheimer. "An fMRI Investigation of Race-Related Amygdala Activity in African-American and Caucasian-American Individuals." *Nature Neuroscience* 8, no. 6 (2005): 720–722; Kubota, J.T., M.R. Banaji, and E.A. Phelps. "The Neuroscience of Race." *Nature Neuroscience* 15, no. 7 (2012): 940–948.

CHAPTER 4: THE POLITICS OF SCIENCE

69 **In 2008, Luigi:** Cavalli-Sforza, Luigi Luca. *Genes, Peoples, and Languages.* University of California Press, 2000; Li, J.Z., et al. "Worldwide Human Relationships Inferred from Genome-Wide Patterns of Variation." *Science* 319 (5866) (2008): 1100–1104.

75   **As one former editor:** Phimister, Elizabeth. "Medicine and the Racial Divide." *New England Journal of Medicine* 348 (2003): 1081–1082.

75   **Labels such as Asian:** Panofsky, Aaron, and Catherine Bliss. "Ambiguity and Scientific Authority: Population Classification in Genomic Science." *American Sociological Review* 82, no. 1 (2017): 59–87.

CHAPTER 5: GENETICS, IQ, AND BEHAVIOR

83   **In *The Mismeasure of*:** Staub, Michael E. *The Mismeasure of Minds: Debating Race and Intelligence Between* Brown *and* The Bell Curve. Studies in Social Medicine Series. University of North Carolina Press, 2018.

83   **Whether promoting racism:** Jensen, Arthur R. "How Much Can We Boost IQ and Scholastic Achievement?" *Harvard Educational Review* 39, no. 1 (1969): 1–123.

83   **As Aaron Panofsky:** Panofsky, Aaron. *Misbehaving Science: Controversy and the Development of Behavior Genetics.* University of Chicago Press, 2014.

84   **Soon after, in the mid-1990s:** Herrnstein, Richard J., and Charles Murray. *The Bell Curve: Intelligence and Class Structure in American Life.* Free Press, 1994.

84   **In his most recent:** Carlson, Tucker, host. "Tucker Carlson Today." Interview with Charles Murray. Fox Nation, June 16, 2021.

85   **research shows that IQ:** Pietschnig, J., and M. Voracek. "One Century of Global IQ Gains: A Formal Meta-Analysis of the Flynn Effect (1909–2013)." *Perspectives on Psychological Science* 10, no. 3 (2015): 282–306.

85   **Likewise, decades of studies:** Dickens, W.T., and J.R. Flynn. "Black Americans Reduce the Racial IQ Gap: Evidence from Standardization Samples." *Psychological Science* 17, no. 10 (2006): 913–920; Rindermann, H.D., David Becker, and Thomas R. Coyle. "Survey of Expert Opinion on Intelligence: Causes of International Differences in Cognitive Ability Tests." *Frontiers in Psychology* 7 (2016): 399.

86   **The left-leaning Urban:** Kronstadt, Jessica. "Genetics and Economic Mobility." Urban Institute, Apr. 2, 2008. https://www.urban.org/research/publication/genetics-and-economic-mobility.

87   **While very few of these studies:** Callaway, Ewen. "'Gangsta Gene' Identified in US Teens." *New Scientist*, June 19, 2009. https://www.newscientist.com/article/dn17337-gangsta-gene-identified-in-us-teens/.

88   **Some have even advocated:** Raine, Adrian. "Opinion: Unlocking Crime Using Biological Keys." CNN, 2013.

89 **Photofits have been used:** "DNA May Change Killer Profile." ABC News, 2003; Randerson, James. "DNA, the Second Revolution." *The Guardian*, Apr. 27, 2003. www.theguardian.com/uk/2003/apr/27/ukcrime7.

90 **Today, even as new:** Diskin, Megan. "DNA May Help Identify 1980 Ventura, Kern County Murder Victims." *Ventura County Star*, June 12, 2018; Johnson, Thaddeus L. "Police Facial Recognition Technology Can't Tell Black People Apart." *Scientific American*, Apr. 1, 2024. www.scientificamerican.com/article/police-facial-recognition-technology-cant-tell-black-people-apart/.

92 **As lead scientist Danielle:** Wade, Nicholas. "In 'Enormous Success,' Scientists Tie 52 Genes to Human Intelligence." *The New York Times*, May 22, 2017. www.nytimes.com/2017/05/22/science/52-genes-human-intelligence.html.

94 **"They're dreaming about another":** Adler, Simon, host. "G: Unnatural Selection." Radiolab, WNYC Studios, July 25, 2019. https://radiolab.org/podcast/g-unnatural-selection/transcript.

95 **Intelligence geneticist Robert:** Callaway, Ewen. "The Promise and Peril of the New Science of Social Genomics." *Nature* 574 (2019): 618–620.

95 **Once you have the genes:** Toynbee, Polly. "Psychologist on a Mission to Give Every Child a Learning Chip." *The Guardian*, Feb. 18, 2014. www.theguardian.com/education/2014/feb/18/psychologist-robert-plomin-says-genes-crucial-education.

96 **In her book *The Genetic*:** Harden, Kathryn Paige. *The Genetic Lottery: Why DNA Matters for Social Equality*. Princeton University Press, 2021.

97 **"I'm not looking for a school":** Lewis-Kraus, Gideon. "Can Progressives Be Convinced That Genetics Matters?" *The New Yorker*, Sept. 13, 2021.

CHAPTER 6: MAKING A BUSINESS OF RACE

107 **But policy analyst:** TallBear, Kim. *Native American DNA: Tribal Belonging and the False Promise of Genetic Science*. University of Minnesota Press, 2013.

107 **A study conducted by NIH:** Walajahi, Hina, David R. Wilson, and Sara Chandros Hull. "Constructing Identities: The Implications of DTC Ancestry Testing for Tribal Communities." *Genetics in Medicine* 21, no. 8 (2019): 1744–1750.

109 **Alondra Nelson has:** Nelson, Alondra. "The Factness of Diaspora." in *Revisiting Race in a Genomic Age*, edited by Barbara A. Koenig et al., 253–268. Rutgers University Press, 2008.

109 **Nelson warns that:** Nelson, Alondra. *The Social Life of DNA: Race, Reparations, and Reconciliation After the Genome.* Beacon Press, 2016.

110 **Law professor and sociologist:** Roberts, Dorothy E. *Fatal Invention: How Science, Politics, and Big Business Re-create Race in the Twenty-first Century.* The New Press, 2011.

111 **"They often feel like":** Elspeth Reeve, "Alt-Right Trolls Are Getting 23andMe Tests to 'Prove' Their Whiteness." *Vice*, Oct. 8, 2016. www.vice .com/en/article/vbygqm/alt-right-trolls-are-getting-23andme-genetic-tests -to-prove-their-whiteness.

111 **Testing for Whiteness:** Roth, Wendy D., and Biorn Ivemark. "Genetic Options: The Impact of Genetic Ancestry Testing on Consumers' Racial and Ethnic Identities." *American Journal of Sociology* 124, no. 1 (2018): 150–184; Panofsky, Aaron, and Joan Donovan. "Genetic Ancestry Testing Among White Nationalists: From Identity Repair to Citizen Science." *Social Studies of Science* 49, no. 5 (2019): 653–681.

113 **As one test taker:** Mitt, Alexandros, Savvas Zannettou, Jeremy Blackburn, and Emiliano De Cristofaro. "'And We Will Fight for Our Race!' A Measurement Study of Genetic Testing Conversations on Reddit and 4chan." *Proceedings of the International AAAI Conference on Web and Social Media* 14, no. 1 (2020): 452–463.

118 **The latest systematic reviews:** Lewis, Brianne E., and Akshata R. Naik. "A Scoping Review to Identify and Organize Literature Trends of Bias Research Within Medical Student and Resident Education." *BMC Medical Education* 23 (2023); Vela, Monica, Amirachi Erondu, Nichole Smith, Monica Peek, James Woodruff, and Marshall Chin. "Eliminating Explicit and Implicit Biases in Health Care: Evidence and Research Needs." *Annual Review of Public Health* 43 (2023): 477–501.

118 **Analyses of medical education:** Tsai, Jennifer. "What Role Should Race Play in Medicine?" *Scientific American*, Sept. 12, 2018.

CHAPTER 7: DECONSTRUCTING RACE

122 **Studies have found that adverse:** Aroke, E.N., et al. "Could Epigenetics Help Explain Racial Disparities in Chronic Pain?" *Journal of Pain Research* 12 (2019): 701–710; Rubin, L.P. "Maternal and Pediatric Health and Disease: Integrating Biopsychosocial Models and Epigenetics." *Pediatric Research* 79, no. 1–2 (2016): 127–135.

122 **Epigenetic studies of:** Geronimus, Arline T., et al. "The Weathering

Hypothesis as an Explanation for Racial Disparities in Health: A Systematic Review." *Ethnicity & Disease* 29, no. 1 (2019): 119–122.

124 **One extremely compelling:** Fausto-Sterling, Anne. "The Bare Bones of Race." *Social Studies of Science* 38, no. 5 (2008): 657–694.

132 **Here I turn to Troy:** Duster, Troy. "Feedback Loops in the Politics of Knowledge Production." In *The Governance of Knowledge*, edited by Nico Stehr, pp. 139–160. Transaction Publishers, 2004.

133 **As Nelson explains:** Nelson, Alondra. *Body and Soul: The Black Panther Party and the Fight Against Medical Discrimination*. University of Minnesota Press, 2011.

CHAPTER 8: THE REALITY OF RACE

140 **As sociologist Ruha:** Benjamin, Ruha. *Viral Justice: How We Grow the World We Want*. Princeton University Press, 2022.

FURTHER READING

CHAPTER 1: A BRIEF HISTORY OF RACE

Bernasconi, Robert, and Tommy L. Lott, eds. *The Idea of Race*. Hackett Publishing Company, 2000.
A collection of essays on race from leading Enlightenment thinkers.

Gould, Stephen Jay. *The Mismeasure of Man*. W. W. Norton, 1981.
A book on scientific racism in the nineteenth and twentieth centuries.

Graves, Joseph L. *The Race Myth: Why We Pretend Race Exists in America*. Dutton, 2005.
A book on the origin and persistence of the race myth in America.

Yudell, Michael. *Race Unmasked: Biology and Race in the Twentieth Century*. Columbia University Press, 2014.
A book on how sciences like genetics have created, contested, and perpetuated race.

CHAPTER 2: THE GENOMICS OF RACE

Reardon, Jenny. *Race to the Finish: Identity and Governance in an Age of Genomics*. Princeton University Press, 2004.
A book on the rise and fall of the Human Genome Diversity Project.

Reynolds, Joel Michael, and Erik Parens, eds. "For 'All of Us'? On the Weight of Genomic Knowledge." Special Report, Hastings Center Report 50, no. S1 (2020).
A collection of articles on the use of race in precision medicine.

Williams, Johnny E. *Decoding Racial Ideology in Genomics*. Lexington Books, 2017.
A book about genomic science's fixation on race.

CHAPTER 3: SEEING AND THINKING RACE

Eberhardt, Jennifer L. *Biased: Uncovering the Hidden Prejudice That Shapes What We See, Think, and Do*. Viking, 2019.
A book that discusses the vast social implications of implicit bias research.

Gilroy, Paul. *Against Race: Imagining Political Culture Beyond the Color Line*. Harvard University Press, 2000.
A book on racialism.

Lee, Orville, and Sarah Daynes. *Desire for Race*. Cambridge University Press, 2008.
A book on the social psychology of perceiving race.

CHAPTER 4: THE POLITICS OF SCIENCE

Dauda, Bege, Santiago J. Molina, Danielle S. Allen, Agustin Fuentes, Nayanika Ghosh, Madelyn Mauro, Benjamin M. Neale, Aaron Panofsky, Mashaal Sohail, Sarah R. Zhang, Anna C.F. Lewis. "Ancestry: How Researchers Use It, and What They Mean by It." *Frontiers in Genetics* 14 (2023): 1044555.
An article on the ways that geneticists conceptualize ancestry.

Duster, Troy. *Backdoor to Eugenics*. 2nd ed. Routledge, 2003.
A book on genomic initiatives and the resurgence of eugenics.

Saini, Angela. *Superior: The Return of Race Science*. Beacon Press, 2019.
A book on how modern sciences like genetics and intelligence research are producing new notions of race.

CHAPTER 5: GENETICS, IQ, AND BEHAVIOR

Broscious, Courtney, and Rashawn Ray. "Dismantling Biological Race and Genetic Essentialism Narratives." *Sociology Compass* 15, no. 9 (2021): 1–14.
An article on genetically deterministic notions of race in sociogenomics.

Carlson, Jedidiah, et al. "Counter the Weaponization of Genetics Research by Extremists." *Nature* 610, no. 7932 (2022): 444–447.
An op-ed by geneticists who suggest ways to fight White supremacist misuses of genetic science.

Martschenko, Daphne. "Sociogenomics and Social Responsibility." *BioSocieties* 17, no. 2 (2022): 321–344.
An article on how to conduct responsible sociogenomic research.

Robinson, Gene E., Rina Bliss, and Matthew E. Hudson. "The Genomic Case Against Genetic Determinism." *PLOS Biology* 22, no. 2 (2024): E3002510.
An article on battling genetic determinism in sociogenomic research.

CHAPTER 6: MAKING A BUSINESS OF RACE

Inda, Jonathan Xavier. *Racial Prescriptions: Pharmaceuticals, Difference, and the Politics of Life.* Routledge, 2014.
A book on race-based medicine.

Kahn, Jonathan. *Race in a Bottle: The Story of BiDil and Racialized Medicine in a Post-Genomic Age.* Columbia University Press, 2012.
A book that provides a history of BiDil.

Saperstein, Aliya, Sasha Shen Johfre, and Jill A. Hollenbach. "Measuring Race and Ancestry in the Age of Genetic Testing." *Demography* 58, no. 3 (2021): 1003–1027.
An article on how genetic tests change how we should measure race.

CHAPTER 7: DECONSTRUCTING RACE

DeGruy, Joy. *Post Traumatic Slave Syndrome: America's Legacy of Enduring Injury and Healing.* Uptone Press, 2005.
A book on social weathering of descendants of formerly enslaved people.

Menakem, Resmaa. *My Grandmother's Hands: Racialized Trauma and the Pathway to Mending Our Hearts and Bodies.* Central Recovery Press, 2017.
A book on epigenetic weathering due to racism.

National Academies of Sciences, Engineering, and Medicine. *Using Population Descriptors in Genetics and Genomics Research: A New Framework for an Evolving Field.* National Academies Press, 2023.
A report on best practices for labeling populations in genetic science.

CHAPTER 8: THE REALITY OF RACE

Benjamin, Ruha. *Race After Technology: Abolitionist Tools for the New Jim Code.* Polity Press, 2019.
A book about algorithmic bias in the age of artificial intelligence.

Kampourakis, Kostas. *Ancestry Reimagined: Dismantling the Myth of Genetic Ethnicities.* Oxford University Press, 2021.
A book about new ways of classifying humans in terms of genetics.

Morning, Ann. *The Nature of Race: How Scientists Think and Teach About Human Difference.* University of California Press, 2011.
A book on how to conceptualize race in the age of genomics.

INDEX

Norton Shorts

BRILLIANCE WITH BREVITY

W. W. Norton & Company has been independent since 1923, when William Warder Norton and Mary (Polly) D. Herter Norton first published lectures delivered at the People's Institute, the adult education division of New York City's Cooper Union. In the 1950s, Polly Norton transferred control of the company to its employees.

One hundred years after its founding, W. W. Norton & Company inaugurates a new century of visionary independent publishing with Norton Shorts. Written by leading-edge scholars, these eye-opening books deliver bold thinking and fresh perspectives in under two hundred pages.

Available Winter 2025

Imagination: A Manifesto by Ruha Benjamin

What's Real About Race?: Untangling Science, Genetics, and Society by Rina Bliss

Offshore: Stealth Wealth and the New Colonialism by Brooke Harrington

Fewer Rules, Better People: The Case for Discretion by Barry Lam

Explorers: A New History by Matthew Lockwood

Wild Girls: How the Outdoors Shaped the Women Who Challenged a Nation by Tiya Miles

The Moral Circle: Who Matters, What Matters, and Why by Jeff Sebo

Against Technoableism: Rethinking Who Needs Improvement by Ashley Shew

Literary Theory for Robots: How Computers Learned to Write by
Dennis Yi Tenen

Forthcoming

Mehrsa Baradaran on the racial wealth gap

Merlin Chowkwanyun on the social determinants of health

Daniel Aldana Cohen on eco-apartheid

Jim Downs on cultural healing

Reginald K. Ellis on Black education versus Black freedom

Nicole Eustace on settler colonialism

Agustín Fuentes on human nature

Justene Hill Edwards on the history of inequality in America

Destin Jenkins on a short history of debt

Quill Kukla on a new vision of consent

Kelly Lytle Hernández on the immigration regime in America

Natalia Molina on the myth of assimilation

Rhacel Salazar Parreñas on human trafficking

Tony Perry on water in African American culture and history

Beth Piatote on living with history

Ashanté Reese on the transformative possibilities of food

Tracy K. Smith on poetry in an age of technology

Daniel Steinmetz-Jenkins on religion and populism

Onaje X. O. Woodbine on transcendence in sports